Honeymoon Forever:

Believe Again in the Power of New and Enduring Love

R. Page Kaufman MA/LCSW

Savant Books and Publications
Honolulu, HI, USA
2021

Published in the USA by Savant Books and Publications
2630 Kapiolani Blvd #1601
Honolulu, HI 96826
http://www.savantbooksandpublications.com

Printed in the USA

Edited by David Shinsato
Cover by Daniel S. Janik
Cover Image by Karin Henseler from Pixabay

13 digit ISBN: 9780999693827

First Edition: May/June 2021
Library of Congress Control Number: 2021938912

Dedication

To all seekers of true and lasting love.

Acknowledgements

Personal thanks to:

- Dr. Joel Popson, MD, for all his excellent medical advice during the writing of this book;

- my professional colleagues and fellow radio show co-hosts, Dr. Anne Ridley, Reverend Phil Strom, and life philosopher, Michael Caditz;

- my dedicated and talented Savant editors, Kathryn Lee and David Shinsato;

- my mentor and teacher, the late, great John Bradshaw;

- my dear parents who modeled for me what lasting love success is all about;

- my life partner, Lovelyn, for all her love, wisdom, and encouragement; and

- my beautiful daughter, Luci, whose advice about love rivals that of some of the greatest minds in the field of love and relationships!

Table of Contents

FOREWORD

When I was first asked to write this foreword, I questioned the notion of eternal love, let alone the idea of a Honeymoon Forever. I thought, "Does anyone still believe in this vision of fantasy and unrealistic expectations?" After all, hadn't most of us been disappointed and let down by our partners and ourselves at one time or another?

Even I, a doctor of human sexuality, who's worked extensively with struggling couples and individuals for the last 20 years, had become skeptical of the Honeymoon Phase's inherent validity. Moreover, I had become unconvinced that meaningful and lasting love could ever be absolute. The fairy tales of childhood that were spoon-fed to all of us never seemed to work out the way we thought they would. It just left people disillusioned, with closed hearts.

Then I read my colleague and friend Robert Page Kaufman's book, *Honeymoon Forever,* which puts forth two pertinent and potent ideas: 1) that true love is attainable, and 2) that this new-found love can last forever.

In this book, the path to fulfilling and enduring love is well laid out, based on Robert's years of work as a psychotherapist and social scientist. *Honeymoon Forever* is also the first work, at least to my knowledge, that delves so exclusively and thoroughly into that exciting and hopeful beginning of love relationships, the Honeymoon Phase.

After having absorbed so many insightful beliefs and ideas, chapter after thought-provoking chapter, this book has made me a true believer in the ongoing process of, and commitment to, the eternal power of fulfilling love.

Even if you feel like you've closed your heart to love, I highly recommend this book as your personal guide on your journey to a *Honeymoon Forever*.

Love and blessings…

- Dr. Anne Ridley, the *Modern Aphrodite*

PREFACE

Through the years, I've noticed patterns in my behavior, especially at the start of my love relationships.

First, there was that inevitable excitement of meeting a new person, followed by that "I can't wait to see her again!" feeling. Then came the hopeful anticipation of the first physical touch with my new love, with an expectation of that love continuing way into the future. But, I've also felt my share of anxiety and apprehension during those times of great expectations. Sure, I was excited, but also a nervous wreck I wanted this new love to last!

There was no mistaking my initial exhilaration and anticipatory excitement as anything other than the hope-filled courting experience known as the Honeymoon Phase of relationships. No, this wasn't about some wild week in Cancun following the marriage ceremony, but something more profound—something with staying power!

I knew the Honeymoon Phase was important, and I wanted to get it right. But, seemingly out of the blue, my euphoria would start to wane, and my hopeful anticipation for true love and expectation of lasting partnership would be doused again and again. I would plummet into disappointment and heartbreak. In short, I was an emotional wreck!

Failure after failure, I realized there was something about this first stage of love that I wasn't understanding, that I just wasn't getting right.

Finally, having had enough of frustration and emotional pain, I arrived at a crossroads and asked myself some pretty important questions: how could I be more mindful during my search for meaningful and lasting love? Once I had found "her," what could I do to help turn this short-term attachment into a successful long-term partnership? What had I learned from these brief encounters, even the ones that ended in disillusionment?

Was there something about the Honeymoon Phase that I needed to better understand?

All of this scrutiny regarding my feelings about love began to really percolate, not just as a psychotherapist, but as someone who wanted to learn from his own life experiences and possibly even share them with others.

And so came the reason for this book.

I began interviewing couples at local restaurants, Starbucks, the park, in line at markets, at the beach—anywhere I could find people willing to talk about their personal encounters with love and their particular Honeymoon Phase experiences. In doing so, I found just about everyone was familiar with the Honeymoon Phase, and just the mention of it would attract lots of attention. During my interviews with couples (almost 200), it wasn't uncommon for others who happened to overhear our conversations to passionately offer their own feedback:

"I know what the Honeymoon Phase is. Everyone knows what it is!"

"It's the first year of a relationship, when you're both way into each other but kind of crazy."

"Oh yeah, the honeymoon phase. That's when everything's all hearts and kisses, but way out of control!"

"The Honeymoon Phase is all about having a lot of hot sex!"
"It never lasts....!"

"Honeymoon Phases are just a bunch of crazy, made up fantasies that usually end up with dead relationships! It's all B.S.!"

Apparently, I had touched a lot of nerves.

Everybody had an opinion about the Honeymoon Phase. But they didn't seem to understand the nuts and bolts, the totality of what it was all about, except for speculative little snippets—mostly guesses.

Furthermore, the Honeymoon Phase seemed to have an overwhelmingly bad rap as just some intense and chaotic experience, mostly sexual and mindless in nature. What I found to be a critical stage of love relationships was too often thought of as something superficial and flighty, a crazy and pointless pursuit, a dead end.

This negative point of view had definitely taken its toll on aspiring lovers, leading them to distrust and overlook the unbridled power and intimate nature of this truly amazing and hopeful first stage of love. I also found that there were an awful lot of people who'd lost their belief in love. They had become cynical, angry and jaded, as if the search for love just wasn't worth it anymore.

Faced with such negativity, I wanted to help restore hope to those disillusioned with romance. I understood the Honeymoon Phase's intrinsic importance as a conduit, a critical stepping-stone on the way to a longer-lasting partnership, and realized no one had ever written a whole book about it.

Perhaps, as an experienced psychotherapist and a true believer in the power of love, I can help reestablish the belief that searching for love is still a worthwhile goal. Successful long-term love isn't just some far-flung fantasy, but something real and absolutely attainable!

I knew this message of hope, going against the grain of a largely cynical world, would be an upward climb. But I have found it well worth the time and effort.

Hopefully, through this book, I'll be able to assist you and your partner in growing to your fullest potential, so that one day you may bask in eternal love, just the way it was meant to be experienced—together.

INTRODUCTION

People struggle with love relationships right from the initial search and well into the future.

Divorce rates are sky-high, the whole idea of the nuclear family is under fire, and lots of people seem more confused than ever about how to begin an intimate relationship, let alone stay in one. And it's no wonder! Love is complicated enough, and the frenzied pace of our highly technological 21st Century doesn't make matters any easier.

So, we ask ourselves: how do we find love, and just as important, how do we keep it alive and well?

I believe that both the problem and the solution start with the powerful and inevitable beginning stage of relationships, widely recognized as the Honeymoon Phase (which I'll refer to as the HMP throughout the rest of this book).

The HMP is just as valid and indispensable as the much sought-after long-term love experience, itself, and is the essential first step on the search and realization of long-lasting love. It's commonly considered by many to be one of the happiest and ecstatic experiences known to man (and woman). For centuries, writers, bards, and poets have touted its positive effect on those experiencing newfound love.

The HMP offers us so many positive feelings and experiences we unceasingly search for: warmth, nurturance, empowerment, sharing, meaning, and the prospect of everlasting love. This fresh and novel experience can be a thrilling time of adventure, spontaneity, and immense learning that can produce genuine feelings of well-being and do wonders for self-esteem. It ultimately embodies the spiritual ideal of truly living and loving in the moment, without the unrealistic and sky-high expectations that have plagued so many well-meaning seekers of love throughout time.

But if we aren't careful, it can also devolve into a disappointing haze of emotional pain. If we don't approach this hopeful time with an open attitude and a basic knowledge, the fulfillment of enduring love is not likely to happen. Lasting partnership will remain elusive and well beyond the grasp of those who sincerely search for love.

This exploration requires some serious consideration in order to adopt a view of the HMP that is more than just "an exhilarating experience." It shouldn't be seen as some frivolous time mindlessly passed in childish fantasies of "perfect love" so often—and unrealistically—portrayed in romance novels and Hollywood movies. It is a necessary rite of passage in both the search for love and the developing relationship that follows. And like any meaningful pursuit, this "new beginning" takes effort, mindfulness, and a heavy dose of patience.

I like to think of the HMP as a friendly gathering in a steamy hot tub where people are glad to be together, happily revealing themselves and exchanging new ideas by way of honest communication. In the safety of the warm, bubbling water, stimulating conversations float about, all in the spirit of spontaneity, healthy curiosity, and a whole lot of fun.

But like the percolating waters of a hot tub, the HMP is not stagnant and unchanging. It's constantly in motion and evolving, varying in depth of emotion and length of time depending on the unique chemistry of the people involved. Like the relationship itself, it must constantly be renegotiated and renewed.

All of us would benefit from the HMP's powerful impact to produce and encourage this continual regeneration. Its creative power can be harnessed and used as a positive love-generating force, a necessary first step to long-term intimacy.

So, with all that in mind, let's begin right at the beginning, by continuing to define and better understand the Honeymoon Phase—that crucial and indispensable starting point on your sacred journey to your Honeymoon Forever.

Enjoy the lovely ride!

CHAPTER 1
The Honeymoon Phase—The Defining Moment

"It's the urge to merge...I'm elated! And I'm always with him! Problems don't matter so much, and the sex is wonderful! For me, it's a euphoric and positive time...maybe even a sign of true love..."

—Susanne

"The communication between the two of you seemed unbelievable, as if you could read each other's minds and anticipate each other's words and feelings. She seemed to remember everything about you and bombarded you with her love and positive feelings about life."

—Herb Goldberg, Ph.D.

Paula and Ben are on their third date. They're dining at an intimate LA restaurant, just after taking in a movie. You can see it in the way they gaze at each other across the candle-lit table. There's some tension present, both appearing to be on their best behavior. They make conversation, attempting to keep away those uneasy moments of silence as Paula occasionally laughs a bit too loud at

Ben's jokes. These two seem to like each other. They're a hopeful couple enveloped in the "Honeymoon Phase."

Excitement, positivity, euphoria, fantastic sex, elation, no worries, time spent together, and even early signs of true love are some of the typical words and feelings expressed by couples to describe the Honeymoon Phase, or HMP.

Sound familiar? It's probably safe to say that most of us, at one time or another, have felt the expectant enthusiasm and powerful emotional pull of the HMP. I know I have!

As is the case with love, few of us have truly been able to define the HMP by any one definition, even though it's talked about, written about, and assigned characteristics both positive and negative. It's an almost mystical experience that often transcends words.

After all, how do we define a state of being as subjective as "love," "happiness," or "freedom?" But make no mistake, the majority of our interviewed couples usually know the HMP when they see it, and when they're in it!

Everyone experiences the HMP differently, but there are a few characteristics across-the-board that are common to most relationships. My goal here is not only to help you be able to spot them, but to provide you with some definitions of the HMP that you can use to help you on your way to lasting love.

So, let's look at some of the underlying characteristics of the HMP experience and a few interesting opinions from some relationship pros.

DUAL DEFINITIONS—TWO SIDES OF THE SAME COIN

Based on my research and my own personal life experiences, here's a definition of the Honeymoon Phase:

The Honeymoon Phase is a positive human phenomenon, a beginning stage of love relationships. It typically commences shortly after one person—of any age, sexual preference, orientation, or spiritual bent—meets another person with the intent to forge an interpersonal connection. Such a connection is not limited by any geographical location or exact length of time.

By this definition, the HMP is:

• An almost universally recognized experience common to most cultures.

• A beginning phase or stage that is vital to most love.

• A spiritual and expansive experience, sometimes almost transcendent, yet practical.

• A hopeful time of connection with another person that always involves mutual intention.

• A shared experience not defined by location or time.

Of course, anyone who's been involved in a Honeymoon Phase knows that no clean-cut definition, like the one above, can completely sum up the actual experience, which can be so physically, emotionally, and spiritually all-encompassing. Terry Gorski—author, public speaker, and consultant in the addiction and behavioral health field—has even described the gravity and power of this first stage of love as "going back to the primal dust."

So let's add to this definition some of the experience, itself:

The Honeymoon Phase is the beginning stage of a love relationship, often characterized by powerful physical and emotional moments, which may include elation, euphoria, infatuation, deep romantic interest, unbridled optimism, coupled with mutual concern, exclusivity, and feelings of strong attraction.

HMP CHARACTERISTICS

Positive feelings of excitement, elation, happiness, hope, sexual attraction typically characterize the HMP, along with higher emotional risk-taking and the tendency to idealize your significant other. Hopeful expectations are usually present and freely expressed between partners in the anticipation that there might be a bright future in store for them.

During the HMP, people feel sexier and more alive. Extra attention is paid to personal hygiene and "looking good." As one of our interviewees reflected, "We're both in our Sunday best." Though, in truth, it almost doesn't matter what one wears. When peering through the rosy lenses of the HMP, little imperfections are often ignored.

Mutual respect and trust abound. Lovers feel emotionally and psychologically safe with one another. There's no reason to suspect betrayal or neglect because everything is so fresh and new. With the HMP, a shared admiration is forged.

Take Brenda, a successful real estate agent. She has been dating Robert, an independent movie producer, for almost 6 months now, and her feelings of admiration for him are still growing. Robert appears to feel the same way. Their positive feelings for one another are a sure sign of the Honeymoon Phase in motion:

Brenda: "I really like him so much! He's so confident and positive about everything!"

Robert: "She's always so sure of herself! She seems so cool under pressure!"

There can also be feelings of amplified joy and lots of shared opportunities for lightness and laughter during those first stimulating encounters with a new love. Life becomes more fun for both, and enjoyment abounds.

These are the good times for Robert and Brenda, as they virtually gushed with shared enthusiasm:

Robert: "We have so much fun together! We're always laughing about something!

Brenda: "Being with Robert is the best! I really love it!"

A true spirit of exploration and openness are some of the

HMP's most notable merits. Each person can sense possibility, even a new sense of creativity that can exist during this jubilant time. Many of the couples often comment that, during the HMP, everything feels brand new, like a miraculous unfolding. Robert and Brenda are no exception:

Robert: "This is all brand new to me, and I'm loving every minute of it!"

Brenda: "I know this might sound corny, but It's like I'm a new flower emerging from the fertile soil of life! It just kind of takes you over. I feel so alive, like I'm being reborn!"

Maybe this feeling of "rebirth" is why there's so much baby talk bantered about during the HMP!

Another couple, Zoey and Terry, both massage therapists, spoke of feeling ecstatic and almost high during the HMP:

Zoey: "It feels so good, like I'm buzzed!"

Terry: "It's like I can't get enough of Zoey!"

During the HMP, there's a curiosity, an initial search for identity as a couple, as well as individuals. Two lovers often strongly identify with each other, like Reggie and Ruby, who just met 3 weeks ago at a singles event:

Reggie: "I know we just met, but it already feels like we're meant for each other."

Ruby: "I have a feeling that Reggie's my soul mate... It's like we belong to each other, like I finally met the One..."

Conversations during the HMP are typically exploratory in nature, as 28 year old Andy says:

"I think each partner is sizing up the other for an eventual long-term relationship. We're looking for things in common. It clears the way for commitment."

Judy and Steve have gone out for a while now, but they're still sincerely curious about each other:

Judy: "I want to know all about him... especially what he likes!"

Steve: "I'll ask her things, like about sports. And now I know she likes sports, just like me!"

Still, the HMP is often seen as a time when even trivial similarities and interests hold almost supreme importance, which may seem comical to outsiders but not to the two involved in the HMP:

Kelly: "You went to college? Me too! And you like Cherry Garcia ice cream the best? So do I!"

Chloe: "You like cats! Wow! That's so great! I have ten!!!"

As we can see by the examples above, there's an overwhelming eagerness to "know the other." Personality traits, basic beliefs, likes, dislikes, and shared values are considered and explored by each prospective lover.

This desire to "know the other" is an unfolding process, one that takes time, effort, vulnerability, and courage—a true act of intimacy in itself!

TIME AND THE HONEYMOON PHASE

One question on everyone's mind seems to be, "How long does a Honeymoon Phase last?"

Though the average HMP seems to last about nine months (incidentally, the time it takes to give birth!), its span can vary greatly between couples. Those that I've interviewed report the HMP lasting anywhere from a few days to a lifetime.

But does it have to end? And if so, when? Some say that the HMP ends after the first argument when initial best behavior can quickly become a thing of the past or when sexual desire diminishes. A great number believe that the HMP dies when deeper personal issues and differences inevitably emerge, or when day-to-day reality sets in.

And yet, a surprising number of my interviewees maintained that the HMP doesn't have to end, that there are always elements of the HMP that they carry into long-term relationships. As one zealous respondent put it, "It may not be the same, like when we first met, but for us, it's not over yet!"

It's inspiring that more than a few of the more "experienced" couples remain adamant that the HMP never has to end, that the fire and passion of the "in love" state can last forever. For them, love never dies.

RELATIONSHIP GURUS AND THE HMP

Now, what do some of the professionals have to say about the HMP? Their views may not only interest you but surprise you, too!

Susan Campbell, a researcher and therapist in the relationship field, has written about the "Five Stages of Relationships." The first stage she describes is the "Romance Stage," where "everything is wonderful, beautiful, fun, and exciting… the need satisfied here is love and belonging."

She states that this first stage (what I call the Honeymoon Phase) is "characterized by its dream-like qualities, fantasies, hopes for the future, the possibilities and the asking of 'what if'…but the stage does allow for the building of a foundation for the relationship in the future." Despite its attributed dream-like nature, the HMP cannot be underestimated.

John Bradshaw, the late world-renowned lecturer on relationships and brilliant cutting-edge thinker in the recovery field, shared his own observations regarding the beginning of love relationships:

"It's going back to primal codependency when two people

view the other as bigger than they are...It's that falling in love stage when you're not in your right mind. And it's oceanic-like. You idealize the other's potential and your own personal potential. Now I have potential to expand and grow into that idealized image of the other. It's really a time when you're one with each other. It's exhilarating and always erotic...Now, the shadow side is hidden during this phase, and you don't have to work that hard at it...Actually, it's really an altered state of consciousness. It's like going back to the Big Bang!"

When I asked Mr. Bradshaw about the positive side of the HMP after one of his incredible lectures, he exclaimed, "I don't mean to present this symbiotic phase as necessarily negative. This period can be a wonderfully positive and creative time for people starting out in relationships."

John Grey, the well-known lecturer and writer of many popular relationship books, weighs in with these ideas regarding the beginnings of love:

"Falling in love is like springtime. We feel as though we will be happy forever. We cannot imagine not loving our partner. It is a time of innocence. Love seems eternal. It is a magical time when everything seems perfect and works effortlessly. Our partner seems to be the perfect fit. We effortlessly dance together in harmony and rejoice in our good fortune."

Psychotherapists Gay Hendricks, Ph.D. and Kathlyn Hendricks, Ph.D. refer to the Honeymoon Phase as the "Romance" stage:

"This is the stage the songs are written about. It's wonderful, energetic, humming with excitement. It's when everything the other person does is magic, and your cells are a-buzz with the limitless possibility of life. For years your unconscious mind has been assembling expectations about what it would take to make you happy. Finally, you have found someone who fits all your pictures."

Agree or disagree, I hope that the opinions offered here can help you understand the HMP and what it means to you.

CHAPTER 2
Coming Attractions and the Four Elements of the HMP

"Attraction represents the starting phase of a love relationship; it is present in all cultures and societies...It is a sudden and unpredictable experience favoring the bonding between two unrelated individuals..."

—Marazziti and Cassano

THE MOMENT OF CONCEPTION—ATTRACTION

When does the HMP begin? Based on research and life experience, the HMP commences when both parties fully acknowledge and openly "own" their mutual attraction for one another. After all, love relationships can't develop or continue when attraction isn't mutually expressed. A lack of feelings sensed by one or both individuals could derail the whole process. This may sound obvious, but attraction might only exist in the mind or heart of one partner. In any event, we'll call the initial emotional pull between two potential lovers "Initial Attraction."

Basic attraction to another person is usually both an emotional and intellectual experience. Even at this starting point, it's never too early to examine this partnering process with your head on straight in preparation for what may follow. Being aware of your personal process of falling in love can help you walk the path of your relationship with more presence, grace, and intention. This gained awareness can assist you in discovering your mistakes and reversing "bad love habits."

At this stage, two people have already met and experienced a "bees to honeylike attraction." This powerful pull may show itself as overt physical attraction (the HMP definitely has its sexy side), but there's also subtlety in budding relationships, including nonverbal cues like body posture, dress, voice quality, laughter and flirty touching. And let's not forget the delicate dance of fragrant scents and other natural smells.

Think of this strong pull as a sort of seductive force that gently (or not so gently) pulls you into a free-flowing river where the current tends to flow down stream, just as the elements of the HMP tend to happen in a fairly predictable way, though not always.

This "Initial Attraction" stage leads into what I like to call the "Four Elements" of the HMP.

THE FOUR ELEMENTS

The four Elements are meant to serve as a general guideline to help you navigate the often-unpredictable waters of the HMP. This cyclical way of viewing the first phase of love also helps reveal one of the greatest secrets to successful relationships.

THE FOUR ELEMENTS OF THE HMP

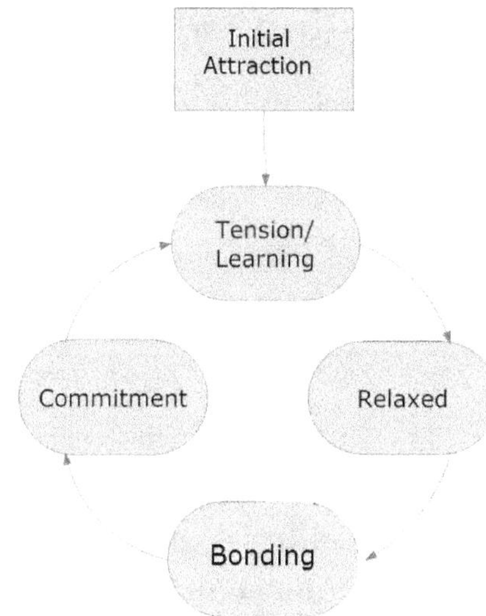

ELEMENT ONE: TENSION

Once attraction has been established, dating usually begins. You've gotten into the same rowboat (or inner tube if that's more your style) and you're both beginning to drift along together, down-river. Just like the unpredictable currents, it's important to note that the speed of the relationship will proceed at its own pace based on the agreement (sometimes unspoken) of the two individuals. Of course, this agreement has to be mutual.

Within this first element, general dating tension may arise and questions may surface, like:

- When and how often should I call?

- Should I wait for them to call?

- Who pays for that first dinner and a movie?

- Should we go for a long walk on the beach or meet at Starbucks?

And who doesn't know about that uncomfortable sexual tension that's almost always there at a first meeting? While he's wondering just how close he can get to her, she may be wondering how close she can let him get! This sort of anxiety isn't necessarily a bad thing, unless it leads to immature or manipulative behavior. Increased tension often goes hand-in-hand with increased excitement, like a storm surge when the river rises and currents begin to swell. This is the powerful energy that drives the HMP.

ELEMENT TWO: RELAXATION

Once the storm has passed, the river calms. And so it is with the Relaxation element of the HMP. Once the tension of the first element begins to subside, you and your partner have a sense that something deeper is opening up. You feel that it's okay to relax into the relationship. Now you're going with the natural flow of the river. This element is usually more experientially comfortable than the Tension element.

There's a gradual loosening of inhibitions, with more relaxed physical contact. This naturally leads to honesty and openness between new couples, a vital aspect of relationship success.

You've found your way to true intimacy, as both you and your partner learn more about each other, move past the petty games that tension can bring, and gently drift toward the tranquil waters of long-term happiness. Here's where you can really begin to enjoy the scenery along the riverbanks—the initial risk has passed.

ELEMENT THREE: BONDING

The third element is all about the bonding process, a main feature of the HMP that can continue on for years into the relationship. This element is the super glue of the HMP that holds the key to strengthening your relationship. It's the effortless moments of deep connection with your partner that build the forward momentum necessary to overcome future obstacles and create positive, enduring patterns of relating.

The bonding process typically includes new rituals and routines, growing physicality, shared admiration and lots of new moments devoted to open and intimate communication. Sex, a potent driver of the HMP, may become more frequent, or it may begin if it hasn't already.

This is also the stage when emotional bonding broadens and more common activities are eagerly shared. Couples build more and more memories together, a shared history is created, and true connection is increasingly experienced. The river widens, and both voyagers experience more enjoyment and ease as they happily drift further down the river.

And all this leads into uncharted waters and to an even deeper connection, namely, Element 4—Commitment.

ELEMENT FOUR: COMMITMENT

By now, both partners are hopefully in a relatively fulfilled state of mind and heart. Possibilities and optimistic planning for the future are all part of this element. Each one's vulnerability is more apparent and will continue to emerge as the HMP progresses.

More emotional risks are taken as future promises are freely made. Goal setting and trust continue to develop and mutual commitment is now solidly established.

You and your partner have become one on your journey as the river flows to the open sea, with eyes wide open and hope in your hearts.

IT'S ELEMENTAL

Like the unpredictable ebb and flow of a river, the four elements may not always occur in the same order, and at the end of the day you'll probably discover that you can't really control or direct any HMP with complete certainty. You can fight against the current, but for the most part never completely control or ultimately tame the river. This is where "going with the flow" is the behavior of choice.

Self-sabotage is a perfect example of fighting against the river's natural flow. The fear of a relationship not working out can easily douse the joy of any promising partnership.

What about over-dependency? This is *not* attraction, but rather a sure way to drown out any promise of healthy commitment, as you'll see in a later chapter.

Another example that highlights the unpredictability of the four Elements is the guy who enthusiastically calls a friend to talk about a first date that ended with a marriage proposal. This excited individual is moving fast, probably too fast, leap-frogging from the Tension stage, right over Relaxation and Bonding, and landing with a big splash into Commitment (not that there's necessarily something wrong with a fast-developing love relationship).

Nevertheless, by immersion into the four Elements, you are now thoroughly engaged in the all-important, potentially life changing process of the HMP.

With all this positive talk, I'd be doing you a real injustice if I didn't talk about the natural waning of the HMP. This is something that must be faced in order for a relationship to continually regenerate and live on far into the future.

Despite this natural tendency for the HMP to wane, you'll want to understand how and why this kind of "death and rebirth" of relationship holds the key to everlasting love.

CHAPTER 3

A Honeymoon Forever—Waning and Renewal

"The same way the thrill of a new car wears off, the thrill of a new relationship wears off, too."

—Evan Marc Katz (Dating Coach)

"It is possible to have a successful relationship and to remain special to each other even after many years of being together. However, you must be willing to cultivate and build your relationship. The couple relationship itself has its own needs and when these are met, the relationship will creatively evolve over time."

—Nancy Wesson, Ph.D.

THE WANING

"Doesn't the Honeymoon Phase always end?"

This question is one that I'm asked all the time, so I'd like to address this proverbial fork in the river right now.

In the cave man days (or cave people if we're being politically correct), an empty nest might've meant certain disaster. Once the kids became self-sufficient and less dependent on their parents' constant attention, they'd leave the familial nest, and there'd no longer be a need for the couple to stay together. It's possible that the waning of the HMP may be a remnant of this very human inclination. Then again, it's nice to think that we are much more than our biological tendencies. Our relationships, and the problems associated with them, are more complex than that.

THE TRIGGERS

HMPs do tend to wane, especially when previously submerged psychological issues or challenges surface—and they often do.

You or your partner may trigger these issues, consciously or unconsciously, often manifesting in the form of arguments. Such disputes might be over things as simple as who cooks dinner and keeping the place clean, or as complex as deep-seated insecurities and intimacy issues stemming from one's past. These "hot-button" issues and their corresponding negative attitudes will creep in and seriously challenge the future outcome of your relationship.

I'll bet you've heard some of these before:

- *"You owe me..."* (Keeping score)

- *"This just doesn't seem to be doing it for me anymore."* (General disillusionment)

- *"Not tonight...I'm not feeling well."* (Less sex)

- *"I always feel so distracted when I'm around him now..."* (Partner's company no longer brings as much pleasure)

• *"He never does those sweet little things for me like he used to..."* (Less niceties and attentiveness)

• *"We never get away anymore."* (Less adventure time)

• *"He never used to get drunk in front of my parents!"* (Good behavior wanes)

• *"Is this really who I want in my life? Did I make a mistake?"* (Doubt creeps in)

• *"If she could just get rid of that awful laugh. Who knew?"* (Finding faults)

• *"She's never willing to compromise. She did before!"* (Power struggles appear)

• *"He's such a slob! Funny how it never bothered me before..."* (Resentments emerge)

• *"I'm not into dealing with your childhood abuse issues!"* (Bringing up the past)

One of my clients began having difficulties with her relationship, after bringing up some past abuse issues to her partner. His response was to withdraw and emotionally shut down. This barrier that he built between them almost destroyed their once promising relationship until he was finally able to admit that her disclosures had brought up his own childhood trauma. Once they made it to a common ground of understanding, they were able to move ahead with the relationship.

These psychological triggers, even the small stuff, can turn into deal breakers at any stage of a relationship. Fear of commitment, inability to be open to differences, and even deception may signal the end.

THE SIGNS

Nevertheless, it is still true that the initial magic of the HMP tends to wane, and even faster if you or your new partner aren't acting as fully involved participants. Things can quickly become less exciting, less spontaneous, and really stall out.

Here are some signs that your Honeymoon Phase is waning:

- Minute details take the place of openness and creativity, sexual enjoyment diminishes, and criticism increases.

- Many people feel a loss of independence and a gnawing sense of relationship claustrophobia with exasperated statements like, "She never lets me have any time to myself!"

- Heated arguments flare up when little, trivial things or expectations, once overlooked, now take front and center.

• One person becomes more dependent while the other pushes away.

• Insecurities surface: "He's always staring at other women."

• One or both become more defensive as partners begin to notice each other's character flaws.

• Avoidance behaviors take place.

• Communication and time spent together becomes less frequent.

• Eye contact, handholding, hugs, kisses, and other signs of affection decrease.

• Chivalry becomes less important as partners begin to care less about looking good for the other, and bad habits are no longer hidden.

• Partners listen less and become more easily distracted.

• Red flags are belatedly noticed: "I can't believe I didn't see this coming!"

• Differences that were suppressed are revealed. Nothing is left to the imagination. Now, it's all out in the open.

The waning may've begun, but if this natural tendency is understood for what it is, it can be headed off at the pass. This is because every emerging issue, opinion or attitude, positive or negative, offers a great opportunity to actually grow your relationship.

When challenges signal a waning HMP, fear not. There's always a chance to re-create or renew the magic that made it bloom in the first place. There may be an unsettling shift of the tides—but usually for the better.

THE RENEWAL

Sharing the personal challenges that come up with your partner is always a risk that requires courage and a willingness to acknowledge that the relationship has evolved to the next level. This kind of openness keeps it moving forward.

Remember, I've been talking about the HMP as a process that requires attention, knowledge, and forward momentum.

In the words of Woody Allen, spoken in his Academy Award-winning film, *Annie Hall*:

"I think a relationship is like a shark. It has to constantly move forward or it dies."

Well said, Woody. There's a positive side to relationship turbulence, because everything that arises, at any stage of love, offers an opportunity to renew and move it forward—even the troubles of a waning HMP.

A HONEYMOON FOREVER

The HMP, under most circumstances, and with right-minded effort, can last a very long time. The trick, though, is not to deny that HMPs wane, but rather to keep the process moving along. And with this effort, the HMP moves forward, just like that free-flowing river, unrestricted by time and space.

The river has always been known as the symbol of interconnectedness, constant change, and the eternal. Viewed through this same lens of meaning the Honeymoon Phase, like the ever-changing and sometimes meandering river, is the path to enduring relationship happiness.

In the following chapters, I hope to shed light on the issues that can stifle the flow of any HMP, and most importantly how you can overcome these potential river blockages.

CHAPTER 4
The Honeymoon Phase—A Couple's Eye View

"The intense happiness of our union is derived in a high degree from the perfect freedom with which we each follow and declare our own impressions"

—George Eliot

It's fairly easy for us professionals working in the human development field to sit back and comfortably comment on human phenomena such as the Honeymoon Phase.

But what about the responses from people not actively engaged in the field of relationship research? Those with first-hand knowledge who are actually *in* the HMP?

How do they feel about this crucial stage, and what perspectives can they share with us?

AN INTIMATE CASE STUDY—DON AND REBECCA

I interviewed Don, a mortgage broker in his early forties, at a crowded West Los Angeles restaurant. He was sitting side-by-side in a booth with his new love, a middle school teacher in her early 30s, named Rebecca. This was a truly handsome couple in the prime of their lives. I couldn't help but notice their shared exuberance, arms wrapped tightly around each other, full of smiles and laughing away. They were even sharing each other's food!

They seemed to glow with admiration for one another as I approached them for an interview, which they gladly accepted. I noticed their infectious sense of joy, excitement, and hope as they spoke intelligently and openly with me about the different aspects of the HMP they were currently experiencing.

THE INTERVIEW

Here are some revealing excerpts from their very own HMP story:

Q: So how do you define the Honeymoon Phase? Just what is it?

Rebecca: "Well, for me, it's a spiritual kind of thing. I think the Honeymoon Phase is all about the beginning, the start of true love together. It's not something false or meaningless. For me, it's an important time when two people seem to think so much alike, and start to create a real mental union, a spiritual union. I know Don's willing to join me, to get to know me, and to really connect with me."

Don: "I think it's when you fall in love, and you can see yourself in the other—the good and the bad. It's when you both obviously like each other even though you don't really totally know that person yet. You don't know what might get on your nerves. And I think there's a tendency to think the other person is perfect when you're in the Honeymoon Phase. But as it goes along, I think you find out things about their personality, some good, some not so good."

Rebecca: "Yeah, I think that's true. But what I like is that we have a chance to learn from each other as the Honeymoon Phase moves along, you know, about how to build trust with each other and work on our relationship skills. For me, the Honeymoon Phase is really a spiritual thing."

Don: "True, it's pretty spiritual for me, too. And I'll tell ya, this isn't my first Honeymoon Phase. But I think I've learned a lot about myself from my other experiences. At least for me, it gets better each time because I try to pay attention to what's really going on. I'm trying to stay out of the fantasy and deal with the reality that's right in front of me. Of course, I hope this is the last one I go through." (He kisses Rebecca on the nose. She smiles at him.)

Rebecca: "It just feels like total harmony. It feels peaceful and kind of wonderfully exciting all at the same time. Now I can share my emotions with Don that I normally wouldn't share with others. And I guess I feel freer to be myself, you know, more open."

Don: "Me, too…But I have to admit, I'm also on my best behavior. But I think the Honeymoon Phase definitely signals the start of something good. There's that feeling of hope for a long future together. It's about possibilities…"

Rebecca: "Yeah, I like that… (They kiss.) And I think I'm generally more productive in all parts of my life when I'm in the Honeymoon Phase. I'm definitely happier at work and get more things done since I met Don. I'm actually more creative and not so bogged down with stuff about loneliness or self-pity, or why I'm not in a relationship. I feel really connected to Don. It's nice to finally have someone like that in my life. I like the feeling. It helps with my potential, and it makes me want to take better care of myself." (Adoring looks from Don)

Don: "Absolutely. But, we're definitely into each other. I guess I'm not so interested in the possible red flags or what might go wrong. It's just moving along so great."

Rebecca: "Like we're in harmony with each other."

Don: "So far, I think we're doing great!" (He looks endearingly at Rebecca)

Rebecca: "Yeah, babe, it's like the Honeymoon Phase has a life of its own. I don't have to keep analyzing it. It just flows…"

Don: "For me, too."

Q: What other ways is life different for you when you're in the Honeymoon Phase?

Rebecca: "Well, I guess I do things I wouldn't normally do, like seeing Don when I should be at work!" (She laughs and kisses Don affectionately on the cheek)

Don: "I'd have to say that I probably spend too much time on the phone with Rebecca, like, every day!" (They laugh)

Rebecca: "And those three-hour phone conversations. I love it! But, I also think I give more compliments and little gifts to everybody, not just to Don. I don't know…I think I generally have more appreciation for life and other people. I'm just happier."

Don: "No question. We're always giving little gifts to each other, and I'm not normally a big gift-giver. It's like a mutual appreciation going on, all the time. It's like I'm spending money more freely. (He looks into Rebecca's eyes with love and admiration) She's worth it. Money just becomes less of an issue. What can I say? I'm in love!" (He gives Rebecca another kiss, and they laugh together)

Rebecca: "Me, too! And Don goes out of his way to help me. Right, Donnie? (They kiss) I feel cared for, like someone's really in my corner. It's a feeling that I don't really get from my girlfriends. Usually, we're just complaining about guys being so selfish and into themselves."

Don: "I have to admit that Rebecca's right. There's a lot of negativity out there about the whole man versus woman thing. But Rebecca and I really do help each other, because we're a team. Problems aren't such a big deal now."

Rebecca: "That's true. Challenges and problems seem smaller and easier to overcome now that we're together. Now, we can work things out, and we don't have to feel alone. Now we can face problems together."

Q: What about communication in the Honeymoon Phase?

Don: "Oh, communication. I think it's so important."

Rebecca: "Sure, it's important. And we do spend a lot of time talking together, much more than I'm used to with other people."

Don: "I think because we're still kind of feeling each other out. (Don winks at Rebecca) You know, it's pretty early for us, but we're pretty excited. Usually, I can't wait to talk to Becca."

Rebecca: "Oh, yes! I enjoy talking with Donnie. He's so smart!"

Don: "Well, you are, too, Reb." (They playfully nuzzle)

Rebecca: "And come to think of it, we don't really fight much."

Don: "Yeah, I don't think we've had any big arguments…Yet."

Rebecca: "Yet?" (They both laugh)

Don: "But, we've had our disagreements. I don't think fighting is something you usually find in the Honeymoon Phase. But don't get me wrong, I don't think the Honeymoon Phase is perfect, by any means."

Q: So, do you think there's a negative side to the Honeymoon Phase?

Don: "Maybe. I think there could be a tendency to put each other up on a pedestal. You know, make the other person perfect?"

Rebecca: "I think during the Honeymoon Phase, there's less of a tendency to project psychological wounds onto each other. I know that I have to see Don for who he truly is, not some made-up fantasy of who I want him to be. I need to be careful not to make Don my dad. (She frowns, and Don comforts her) I need to always remember that it's Don that I'm involved with here, not my parent or someone else."

Don: "That's true. I may see some aspects of my mom or dad in Rebecca, but I also need to realize that it's Rebecca I want to get to know."

Rebecca: "And I think there's the tendency to mirror each other's level of health or unhealthiness. A lot of people that haven't done the right work on themselves can easily let their emotions control them, and then the Honeymoon Phase can get pretty mindless and even hedonistic."

Don: "Then again, I think it's important not to over-analyze the relationship. I mean, I'm enjoying this new adventure with Rebecca. And this time, I think I'm doing it in a healthier way. I think I'm seeing this new relationship for what it really is. I mean, I could just ignore Rebecca's negative stuff, but I don't…" (Rebecca turns her head towards Don with an indignant yet lighthearted look)

Rebecca: "Donnie! What negative stuff? Don't you think I'm perfect?"

Don: "See? I know Rebecca's joking around, but I do think we might both tend to look past the negative stuff that might come up later. You know, each person's dark side, what you don't want the other person to know or things you're not too proud of."

Q: ***Do you think that's true for most people in the Honeymoon Phase?***

Rebecca: "Maybe, but I really think too many people go into the Honeymoon Phase without working on themselves, first. I mean, I've been in a lot of therapy over the years in order to learn what makes me tick. You know, my likes, my dislikes, my needs, and what I really want for my life. Too many people go into relationships without using their heads."

Don: "Yeah, I'm one of those people, or I'd like to think I used to be one of those people. But I've done a lot of work on myself. I think I'm more mindful these days, you know, living more in the moment, not arguing with reality so much. The Honeymoon Phase can be a disaster if you don't have your head together, and that's not fair to your partner."

Rebecca: "Yep. I think it's easy to believe that everything's just peaches and cream. That everything's perfect, like nothing can go wrong in the Honeymoon Phase."

Don: "Yeah, that's so true."

Q: So, the Honeymoon Phase can be risky?

Don: "Especially if you don't know what you're doing."

Rebecca: "Definitely."

Don: "Love is a risk."

Rebecca: "But worth it, if you're willing to take that risk."

Q: How does the future fit in with regards to your Honeymoon Phase?

Don: "You want to keep the bonding going on. I think that over time, you develop ways to make it work. It's kind of a mutual thing. But you have to work at it, because you want it to lead somewhere."

Rebecca: "I really think the Honeymoon Phase can lead to something more, even family life, kids, the whole enchilada."

Don: "True. But only if each person does their inner work first. You gotta be willing to really look at yourself."

Rebecca: "I agree. Without that deep personal work, and, believe me, I was in therapy for a long time, there's not much chance for a really long relationship that can lead to something more, like a family, after the Honeymoon Phase."

Don: "So you want kids, Rebecca?"

Rebecca: "Sure, I thought you knew that."

Don: "See? I'm learning something new about Rebecca every day, in every conversation we have. It's all part of the Honeymoon Phase."

Rebecca: "So, do you want kids, Donnie?"

Don: "We'll talk after the interview, honey." (They both laugh and hug)

A "COUPLE" OF IMPRESSIONS

This couple, as with many of those I've interviewed, appears to personify many of the basic positive traits and characteristics of the HMP experience. Don and Rebecca have done their "psychological homework." Each one is embarking on the HMP in a conscious way with eyes wide open.

During my brief time with Don and Rebecca, there was an almost palpable feeling of aliveness, excitement, and great expectations emanating from this happy couple. I heard the typical pet names and experienced their adrenaline-like surge of optimism, as well as thoughtful and candid responses to my probing and sometimes challenging questions. This exuberant couple appeared to be so thoughtful with their responses, and at times, seemed to embody the creative influences of the muses.

I noticed a positive spirit of non-judgmental communication, an overwhelming acceptance of the other, and a flexible and mutually accepting behavior. There was a pioneering spirit of openness, a readiness to be vulnerable and transparent with one another, to share one's true self, and also a refreshing willingness to honestly acknowledge the possible pitfalls of the HMP. Both of these new lovers were able to speak about the other's shortcomings, recognizing that peoples' dark sides tend to be more hidden during the HMP.

There was little conflict, yet occasional disagreements, which were usually deflected with a healthy show of humor. True, both appeared to be on their best behavior, but they seemed in tune with each other, a kind of "collective synchronization." The overwhelming attention and affection freely given to the other was touching to observe, yet not at all trite, and the spiritual connection between these two appeared to be very strong, like that of soul mates, finally together.

All in all, I observed a true potential for Rebecca and Don to have an exciting and successful relationship, a shining example of the Honeymoon Phase at its flourishing best!

CHAPTER 5
Words of Love

"Love is an irresistible desire to be irresistibly desired."

—Robert Frost

"Unconditional love really exists in each of us. It is the part of our deep inner being. It is not so much an active emotion as a state of being."

—Ram Dass

"...the essence of our being is Love."

—Dr.Gerald Jampolsky

For eons, the powerful phenomenon of love—certainly an integral part of The Honeymoon Phase—has been poked, prodded, and endlessly examined.

Whether we agree with them or not, virtually everyone seems to have a different perception of love with all its various twists, turns, and thought-provoking terms: eros, agape, philia, romantic love, true love, infatuation, love at first sight, existential yearning.

What an abundance of forms! And each and every one of them has a rightful place within the HMP.

TO LOVE AND BE LOVED

It's in our basic nature to love and be loved. John Bradshaw calls this the "Virtue of Love," a way of being that exultantly exclaims, "I love you because you are you!"

Although a beautiful sentiment, how can we truly investigate such a nebulous and controversial matter as love?

Few of us have been able to speak about love objectively in a way that might allow for complete understanding or reaching any final consensus. And are we talking about love strictly as an emotion or more as a conscious decision? Now, there's a revolutionary thought!

Scientifically speaking, love is known for creating a particular state of mind, usually experienced as something pleasurable. By activating the brain's reward system, the experience of love can produce changes ranging from slight mood elevation to intense pleasure and euphoria, not unlike a drug high.

For some researchers, love is viewed as just another human behavior, an altered state of consciousness primarily dictated by brain chemistry.

To the poets, love is elusive and considered more a matter of the heart than anything having to do with highly educated guys in white lab coats.

And to most of the rest of us, love remains a mystery, seen and experienced as a powerful force of human nature that can move mountains and warm the loneliest souls.

One thing is for sure, the awesome power of love is known to many, throughout all times and in all places, as a potent life energy, something to be seriously reckoned with.

So, let's turn our attention to some of the world's timeless artists. Those love-drunk romantics who've dusted the centuries with word, art and song, overflowing with thoughts about love.

THOSE LOVE-DRUNK ROMANTICS

Prior to modern times, the topic of love was typically relegated to the realm of artists, poets, minstrels and romantically inclined writers.

It's difficult to say anything new about a human phenomenon that some of the world's greatest minds have written and sang about for centuries—individuals like Shakespeare, Colette, Flaubert, Tolstoy, Homer and legions of others too numerous to mention.

Consider these writers and their immortal words of love:

"We are never so defenseless against suffering as when we love."

—Shakespeare

"Love is, of all the passions, the strongest, for it attacks the head, the heart and senses simultaneously."

\- Leo Tolstoy, *Anna Karenina*

"Love is a human emotion that wisdom will never conquer."

—Gustave Flaubert, *Sentimental Education*

"I want nothing from love, in short, but love."

—Colette

"The heart has its reasons that the reason will never know."

—Pascal, *Pensees*

These insightful quotes, penned by these legendary figures, represent a concerted effort to grasp the true meaning of love in a valiant attempt to get their heads wrapped around its many nuances.

Yet, most of these great writers, even the most cynical of satirists, routinely express an almost devout respect for love's formidable influence, timeless mystery, and enormous power, which tragically (and literally) drives them crazy!

C.S. LEWIS

The great Twentieth Century writer and rationalist mystic, C.S. Lewis, wrote about four distinctive types of love, each of which is described as a world unto its own: affection (*storge*), friendship (*philia*), romance (*eros*), and charity (*agape*).

It's also known that he was very drawn to the idea of deific, highly spiritual love as he states, "The human loves can be glorious images of Divine love."

For Lewis, who turned from atheist to Christian, God is intrinsically bound to love.

ERICH FROMM

Erich Fromm, in his classic 1956 work, "The Art of Loving," wrote about love as an artful endeavor, something to be learned and consciously created:

Love is an art, just as living is an art; if we want to learn how to love we must proceed in the same way we have to proceed if we want to learn any other art, say music, painting, carpentry, or the art of medicine or engineering.

For Fromm, the pursuit of love is an active endeavor that involves learning and conscious creativity.

He must've read this book!

GERALD JAMPOLSKY

Bay Area psychiatrist, Gerald Jampolsky, in his simple yet incredibly popular book, *Love is Letting Go of Fear*, writes about his highly humanistic view of love. He acknowledges the intrinsic value of love and also how it can only be derailed by fear:

"Love is the total absence of fear. Love asks no questions. Its natural state is one of extension and expansion, not comparison and measurement. Love, then, is really everything that is of value, and fear can offer us nothing because it is nothing."

Dr. Jampolsky goes on to talk about love as ever-changing, something to be freely offered, with no expectations:

The law of love is based on abundance... When we give our love unconditionally to others with no expectations of return, the love within us extends, expands, and joins."

But despite our deep desire for love, we often let fear take over, without even knowing it, which then blocks our ability to create a conscious space for lasting partnership.

So, what's the answer?

Jampolsky would undoubtedly encourage us to cultivate ways of being that render us less fearful and therefore more receptive to love. In other words, love more and fear less.

FROM THE ROAD LESS TRAVELED

In Dr. Scott Peck's brilliant blockbuster book, *The Road Less Traveled*, he describes love as "the will to extend one's self for the purpose of nurturing one's own or another's spiritual growth." What a wise and refreshing definition of love!

He goes on to describe romantic love, falling in love, and infatuation as something very different from true love. Dr. Peck designates falling in love as temporary. It isn't real love, but rather:

> *...a manifestation of love, a form of intimacy that is sexually motivated, effortless, a sudden collapse of ego boundaries, an escape, an act of regression, undisciplined, an instinctual component of mating behavior, the explosive pouring out of oneself into the beloved, an end*

to loneliness, a trick that our genes pull on our otherwise perceptive mind to hoodwink or trap us into marriage.

Quite an astute and relevant mouthful, don't you think?

He continues:

"The feeling of ecstatic lovingness that characterizes the experience of falling in love always passes. The honeymoon always ends. The bloom of romance always fades."

But does this flowering of romance *always* have to fade? Although I appreciate Dr. Peck's take on love, I disagree with him on this particular point.

Remember back in Chapter 3, where I talked about the natural waning of the Honeymoon Phase, but also how a love relationship can always be re-created and revitalized?

The bloom of romance never has to fade!

Dr. Peck goes on to define "real love" as an entity containing many more elements and characteristics, including personal integrity, awareness, and the instinctual act of falling in love. He comments on a myriad of requirements and personal attributes needed to attain real love, including: conscious attention, discipline, the risk of rejection, effort, courage, commitment, intellect, and a healthy sense of separateness.

For him, real love is not an act of conformity, but instead a natural extension of the self, an act of will, a responsible choice. Real love doesn't mean self-sacrifice, a momentary feeling, but rather something objective, enduring, spiritual, yet intangible and sometimes even confusing. True love is about humility, meaning, and intention.

LOVE—JOHN AND ESTELLE'S POV

John Bradshaw had his own unique way of laying out the path to Dr. Peck's notion of "real love," calling the process "The Four Stages to Mature Love." His first stage, or "love stage," is akin to Peck's idea of romantic love, and most closely resembles the HMP experience.

Similar to Bradshaw's first stage, psychotherapist Estelle Frankel remarks in her book, *Sacred Therapy,* that:

"...the first awakenings of love, human or divine, are often so powerful that they knock us off our feet. In the magical intoxication of new love, our usual boundaries and defenses are temporarily taken down, and we experience an expanded sense of self."

Bradshaw's second love stage is all about discontent and conflict, when both partners inevitably begin to reflect on past issues, psychic baggage that often stems from family dysfunction or abuse. The intense emotions that often accompany these triggers can cause great disillusionment between lovers, which leads many to believe that their HMP is waning.

Frankel describes this trying time in relationships:

Our early 'romantic idealizations' of our partner are dis-

lodged by reality and ideally are replaced by more integrated and realistic images of him or her. No longer seen as quite so perfect, partners then have to work at creating an enduring relationship that takes each other's strengths and weaknesses into account.

Bradshaw's third stage, or the "counter dependency" stage, reminds us about the time it really takes to achieve a true sense of separateness while maintaining connectedness in a love relationship. This stage of love is about establishing healthy boundaries while finding and experiencing true acceptance of the other, loving the other while knowing about their shortcomings. This stage is based on establishing a more profound sense of intimacy with another, where two individuals don't exist as one, but live like two separate trees independently rooted, whose leaves and branches have grown together. It's about using mindful intention to reinforce a strong bond without sacrificing one's individuality, a conscious preservation of one another's solitude and independence of thought and action.

This is where intimacy and initial connection has a real chance to grow.

According to Bradshaw, this final stage of love, often taking decades, has to do with "mature attachment" and "interdependency." This is where the deepest form of intimacy and relationship longevity dwells, a noble goal for those who seek a happy, love-filled future.

This is the entrance into what Frankel calls "a more integrated and grounded relationship," where the notion of a true "honeymoon forever" gradually evolves into an infinite reality.

THE SCIENCE OF LOVE

For about as long as they've existed, scientists and researchers have attempted to define, understand, illuminate, and validate the concept of love through exhaustive experimentation, brain studies, the use of test subjects, projected images, and other controversial research techniques. Whatever the method, scientists do their professional best to research and explain love.

RELATED RESEARCHERS

Elaine Hatfield, professor of Psychology at the University of Hawaii, and fellow social psychologist (and ex-husband) G. William Walster, in their 1985 book, *A New Look at Love,* characterize love as "a state of intense longing for union with another." Interestingly, they divide love into two distinct types, "passionate love" and "companionate love."

For them, this union is closely associated with fulfillment and ecstasy where, conversely, separation can often bring on feelings of profound emptiness, intense anxiety, and dark despair—a real double-edged sword.

PROFESSOR JANKOWIAK

Dr. William Jankowiak, university professor, anthropologist, and internationally recognized authority on urban Chinese society, defines the love state as:

"'...any intense attraction involving the idealization of another within an erotic context,' which includes a 'desire for intimacy and the pleasurable expectation of enduring for some unknown time into the future.'"

It's clear that Jankowiak is talking about love as a state of being that includes intense attraction, idealization, eroticism, desire, intimacy, pleasure, and expectations of a bright future.

LIFELONG LOVE—A STUDY

A fairly recent Stony Brook University brain study, using MRIs and projected pictures, compared the neural correlations of long-term married and in-love individuals with individuals who had recently fallen in love.

Two researchers closely associated with this 2011 study, Dr. Bianca Acevedo and Dr. Arthur Aron, discovered highly similar brain activity in regions associated with reward, motivation and "desire" in both sets of couples.

Simply stated, they discovered that the older couples could be just as much in love as their younger counterparts, with Dr.Acevedo concluding that "lifelong love is possible".

I'll go even one step farther than the results of this revealing study. I believe that lifelong love is not only possible, but inevitable when allowed to develop over time with focused determination, mutual understanding, tender touches, and an ever-evolving spirituality to light the way. Sounds like a true Honeymoon Forever to me!

LOVE LIKE A RUNAWAY TRAIN

Aside from all the writers, social scientists and researchers, an important question still remains: how can the fiery passion of the HMP be successfully channeled into true and lasting love?

Some think that the passion of the HMP might be described as a runaway locomotive, uncontrollably barreling down the tracks to who-knows-where.

Noted writer and ex-editor of Cosmopolitan Magazine, Helen Gurley Brown, wrote these words:

"Once begun, a love affair is like a train headed through a tunnel...It is absolutely going to go through because it's been programmed to do that back at the station. There is no use trying to control it."

With all due respect to this great modern thinker, I don't quite see eye to eye with her bold and dramatic statement. Call me an optimist, but I believe that love, at its best, is more positive and sublime. There's a critical interplay that can't always be controlled, but can often be shaped and molded to one's own needs and wants.

In fact, finding this delicate balance is the real trick here. The power of new love must be allowed to reveal itself, but you must also have the wisdom and knowledge to help guide it along. Of course, love often shapes us, but we also have some say in what direction it takes in our lives.

LOVE LIKE A RIVER

Our image of a relationship as a flowing river fits much better than something mechanical, like a runaway train. Just like the ever-changing currents of the river, relationships will ebb and flow, yet often open up into something unexpected just around the bend.

The ancient Greek poet Heraclitus once said: "

We never step in the same rivers twice," because as it flows, a river is constantly re-creating itself each moment with ever-unique parts and particles emerging from the same intrinsic whole."

Kind of reminds me of that Disney song, "Just Around the Riverbend," from the movie, *Pocahontas.* Hollywood always loves to get into the act! Nevertheless, I find Heraclitus' statement to be a very wise and timely one, especially as it relates to our discussion of love and relationships.

LOVE, THE HONEYMOON PHASE AND FRACTALS

Heraclitus' river analogy also sheds light on our view of the HMP as a kind of self-perpetuating interaction, much like the modern concept of fractals, where parts of a pattern serve to fuel or sustain the total, overall pattern (have I totally confused you yet?). Like fractals, the HMP is a microcosm of the whole, and so contains within it the seed and the necessary momentum required for a successful lifelong partnership.

Simply put, the HMP is that initial ball of energy that propels and gives life to any quest, subsequent flourishing, and the ultimate sustainment of love.

The early passion of the HMP is the driving force of the love relationship across time, the DNA or blueprint for all future interactions with your partner. This is why I accept the waning of the HMP as something real. At the same time, I believe that the essence of finding and keeping love by way of the HMP is the fuel, the unifying thread that is maintained through every phase of a love relationship.

As long as the waning tendency of the HMP is followed by a renewal of commitment, the soul of any love relationship can be regenerated with the same passion and connection that characterized its humble beginning. And just as a fractal's pattern repeats for eternity, so too must your actions of love in order for the HMP to thrive and continue for life.

A SHORT SUMMARY OF LOVE

Here are a few of my conclusions with regards to this discussion of love:

- Love is something that must be continually reviewed and renewed, where you and your partner continuously change and adapt for the good of the relationship.

- Love is a learned art, a constant reevaluation of what might've changed and what you can do to re-create your connection, your personal, sacred HMP. This requires each person to routinely take stock of self, and determine what love truly means and how it may manifest into the world.

• Love happens in the here and now and is something that exists both in the heavens above and in the innermost recesses of our hearts—love is a spiritual ideal.

Now, if all this talk about love seems too poetic and transcendental for you, you'll probably enjoy the next chapter, which deals with the more scientific aspects of attraction and how it relates to your "Honeymoon Forever."

CHAPTER 6
Love on the Brain—A Layperson's Primer

"Love and romance seem to be one of, if not the most powerful activator of our pleasure center."

—Michael R. Liebowitz, MD

Only in the last twenty years or so have scientists taken on the formidable task of neurobiological research into the mechanisms and pathways of love and its various stages. It's a science still in its infancy.

Many of the assumptions and ideas developed by those in the relationship field have not yet fully been scientifically proven simply because of our current limited understanding of the complexities of the human brain. Using scientific methods to explore such a personal and subjective phenomenon as love with all its nuances hasn't been easy!

Nevertheless, these contemporary ideas and studies related to relationships, bonding, romance and the "in love" state have already helped to shed some light on the all-important gateway to a successful long-term relationship, the HMP—and beyond.

DR. LIEBOWITZ AND THE EVOLUTION OF LOVE

Psychiatrist, Michael R. Liebowitz, writes:

Love is the strongest positive feeling we can have, the strongest arousal of our limbic pleasure center that can be induced by relating to, being with, or thinking of another person...This is something that has evolved in us as a species over many thousands of years, and seems to be nature's way of ensuring that we seek out and form relationships that last at least long enough to reproduce the next generation.

Dr. Liebowitz further notes that falling in love is different from and easier than staying in love. He hypothesized that this difference has to do with the way our brain chemistry works.

Liebowitz indicates two distinct chemical systems that we've evolved for the purpose of relating to the opposite sex. The first, attraction (the "biological magnet"), serves to bring people together—for males and females to become attracted, have sex, and reproduce. The second, attachment (the "biological glue"), serves to keep them together.

These ideas have been carried well into the new millennium, most notably by the work of Dr. Helen Fisher, acclaimed author and anthropologist. Her work, along with that of other neuroscientists, has generated a wealth of new information using brain scanning, MRIs, and conducting research into the brain chemistry of humans and other mammals.

DR. FISHER AND THE 3-EMOTION SYSTEM

Dr. Fisher, in her groundbreaking book, *Why We Love*, provides invaluable information regarding the nature and chemistry of romantic love. She includes a section on how lust, attraction, and attachment—the three "love stage" circuits or emotionally driven tracks—are interconnected, and how they influence each other.

Fisher believes that these three brain circuits are interrelated and closely linked to the brain's emotional system that controls parenting, reproduction, and mating. This connection may lead to sexual feelings (lust) and romantic feelings (attraction), which can in turn lead to deeper commitment (attachment) and a long-term relationship.

Now let's briefly break down this three-part model in order to describe the chemistry of love as it relates to the HMP.

LUST, ESTROGEN AND TESTOSTERONE

The sex drive represents the most basic of our instinctual behaviors. Libido is highly variable within human individuals and cultures, yet the main purpose, at least on a biological level, is to initiate the mating process. This craving for sexual gratification is primarily mediated by the sex hormones, estrogen and testosterone.

In women, sexual arousal and response is associated with the presence of increased estrogen, which can work in tandem with testosterone. In menopausal women, administration of estrogen plus testosterone may provide greater psychological health, including increased sexual arousal and orgasm potential.

Higher testosterone levels are positively related to greater sexual interest. When men and women receive testosterone injections for lack of sexual desire, they report an increased sex drive, but not necessarily an upsurge of those "falling in love" feelings.

In men, sexual arousal and libido are more directly associated with the presence of testosterone. However, higher levels of testosterone can actually drive down the hormones related to attachment. Men with high testosterone levels reportedly marry less, have more adulterous affairs, commit more spousal abuse, and divorce more often.

As a man's marriage becomes less stable, his levels of testosterone may rise, finally reaching its apex at the time of divorce. So, it may just be that single, unattached, un-bonded men typically have higher levels of testosterone than married men. Conversely, men who do marry tend to have lower levels of testosterone.

Now we can understand the over-the-top behaviors of those drama-seeking "high testosterone" Don Juans of the world and their lusty pursuits of unsuspecting women. Perhaps these “hot to trot” lovers are embroiled in some unconscious attempt to satisfy a chemical need as they invest themselves in one short-term tryst after another. Whatever the case may be, these very randy guys are engaging in multiple affairs that certainly don't qualify as HMPS!

An optimistic note for the women: despite these troubling correlations, testosterone, even lots of it, is still usually a good thing for your man because it promotes the confidence and friskiness that can spice up any love relationship.

But beware, too much or too little testosterone can have a negative effect on your relationship. Just look at those wild and crazy Don Juans!

THOSE SMELLY PHEROMONES!

We know how smells can affect human sexual desire through perfumes, colognes, and natural body odors. This olfactory attraction is usually caused by pheromones, the chemicals that are secreted by glands throughout the body. For all we know, we may be choosing our mates based on an unconscious, primitive sense of smell that bypasses the parts of our brain that deal with rational decisions.

Dr. Norma McCoy, professor of psychology at San Francisco State, found that subjects exposed to pheromones received significantly more intimate attention, including more hugging, kissing and sexual interaction, which bodes well for relationship longevity.

In fact, pheromones are now being sold commercially to those who want to increase their sexual attractiveness. They're the perfect Xmas stocking stuffers!

ATTRACTION AND THE HONEYMOON PHASE

The second phase, attraction, consists of the emotions and behaviors that represent the classic feelings during the HMP: falling in love, romance, infatuation, and increased passion. Because this phase is characterized by a focus of attention on one preferred partner, Dr. Fisher theorizes that these feelings of attraction evolved in humans to conserve their mating and sexual energy. Evolutionary psychologists and anthropologists see this as an advantage for natural selection and adaptability as a species.

Biochemical research now seems to show that feelings of euphoria, optimism, exhilaration, craving, and increased energy are related to certain neurotransmitters in the brain: dopamine, norepinephrine, and serotonin—the principal initiators and sustainers of love.

DOPAMINE—THE DRIVER

Dopamine is probably the most important brain chemical related to the seeking and craving behaviors associated with the HMP.

This brain chemical increases our ability to focus our attention and precipitates goal-driven behavior. It increases our level of arousal, makes us more alert, and heightens our awareness. It's the "I gotta have it" chemical that motivates us to action, like an animal or a human being seeking food, a safe place, or a potential mate.

Dr. Fisher has correlated at least four characteristics of romantic attraction with elevated levels of dopamine in the brain:

1) Dopamine is so related to goal-oriented motivation that it makes it easy for a prospective partner to "put their blinders on," overlooking the other's negative qualities. It's like placing a new partner up on a pedestal, where they can do no wrong. And as we'll see, this kind of myopic point of view can make things pretty rough, especially if it leads to more negative, obsessive-compulsive behaviors.

2) With higher levels of dopamine, potential partners feel the uniqueness and special quality of their new love. His or her focus on the other becomes almost laser-like, making it almost impossible to

think about anyone else.

3) It's not surprising that a dopamine surge correlates with feelings of euphoria and increased mental activity. Who doesn't think falling in love feels great? It's the ultimate stimulant and antidepressant, all rolled into one.

4) Dopamine is associated with an almost amphetamine-like quality related to reward, arousal, and pleasure. It's not unlike chocolate, cocaine, food, or money, with the same regions of the brain centers being affected. The anticipated excitement of new lovers being together is the dopamine talking!

NOREPINEPHRINE—DOPAMINE'S BABY BROTHER

Norepinephrine, a chemical similar to dopamine in structure and action, is also responsible for some of the stimulating effects of passion and excitement that are so common to the HMP.

This stimulant is thought to encourage imprinting behavior, the instinctive attachment of babies to their mothers, where following her everywhere becomes the center of their attention—just like involvement in the HMP!

SEROTONIN—ANOTHER CLOSE RELATIVE

The neurotransmitter serotonin, a close chemical relative of dopamine and norepinephrine also seems to play a role in the quest for love.

Recent studies have linked lowered serotonin levels with the obsessive thinking associated with those newly in love, or to the extreme, those romance junkies who can't seem to do anything but obsess about others. So, it would make sense that a higher level of serotonin would help to decrease these crazy-making ruminations.

It's also been theorized that as levels of dopamine and norepinephrine increase, serotonin tends to decrease. That may explain why we think of our love partner more often as the love relationship deepens.

To this day, exactly how serotonin works, interacts, and relates to romantic love is still somewhat of a mystery. In any case, it appears that serotonin plays an active part in love, yet another piece of the whole attraction puzzle.

STRESS AND ATTRACTION

The pursuit of love involves an ongoing process of desire and choice, and a certain amount of stress and tension may come with the territory. Researchers, Tobias Esch and George Stefano, have written about stress as it relates to love and human attachment:

> *In recent reviews on the role of stress in human attachment, it has been discussed that stressors can trigger a search for pleasure, proximity or closeness, i.e.: attachment behaviors...It is surmised that some degree of strong, yet manageable stress may be necessary for very strong bonds to develop...to drive the organism into rebalancing by seeking pleasure through social attachments...Thus, stress and love are interconnected...*

Here, these two researchers remind us that a modicum of stress (the good kind) is often a necessary part of accessing that pleasure. When experienced in a balanced, moderate way, stress can act as an essential motivating factor that can allow us to progress from the attraction level of relationships to long-term attachment.

ATTACHMENT—LET'S BOND!

This brings us to the third and final biological phase of the three-emotion system—attachment. After lust (mediated by estrogen and testosterone), then attraction (dopamine), a successful HMP will often lead to bonding and long-term partnership. Now, for those of you who may want to go even deeper into this complicated but interesting world of the brain's "love" chemicals, here's a closer peek at those substances specifically related to attachment.

OXYTOCIN AND VASOPRESSIN—LET'S CUDDLE!

Oxytocin, affectionately called the "cuddle" hormone, and vasopressin, the same hormones also found in mother-infant bonding, are responsible for that special feeling of happy togetherness found in the attachment stage of love. Oxytocin also enhances eye-gaze and increased empathy in men, boosts trust, reduces fear and anxiety, and increases loyalty and devotion—all important factors for the creation of secure and lasting love relationships.

Because both oxytocin and vasopressin are released in men and women during sexual arousal and orgasm, these chemicals are usually involved in both adult short-term and long-term bonding. Researcher Larry J. Young states, "Perhaps frequent sexual activity stimulates the neural circuits responsible for maintaining the pair bond, preserving and strengthening the partnering bond over time."

As we can see, these powerful brain chemicals are vital to bonding, commitment, and a full sex life as you pass through the HMP on your way to your long-term relationship.

A CONDENSED MAP OF THE HMP

To see how all of this ties together, check out my "Bio Map of the HMP":

Honeymoon Phase => Long-Term Love Relationship

The Four Elements of the HMP—I Initial Attraction, II Tension, III Relaxation, IV Bonding

Brain Chemicals—Pheromones, Dopamine, Oxytocin, Testosterone, Norepinephrine, Vasopressin, Estrogen, Serotonin

The Three Emotion System—Lust, Attraction, Bonding/Attachment

LOVE AND THE BRAIN

British neurobiologists, Andreas Bartels and Samir Zeki, found that those who reported being in love, showed increased activity in areas of the brain while viewing pictures of their partners. These areas overlap with other parts of the brain responsible for cocaine and opiate-induced euphoria. Gazing at photos caused the brain scan to light up the area that helps us detect, perceive, discriminate, anticipate and obtain rewards.

As previously mentioned, this suggests a close neural link between romantic love and euphoric states. The highly charged in-love state may actually reduce the ability for critical judgment when deciding if a partner is true HMP material.

As we noted in an earlier chapter, new lovers tend to idealize their partner. They build them up into super beings, the embodiment of almost god-like perfection. This is a kind of denial—rose-colored-glass thinking verging on pure fantasy. HMP partners often think their newfound love connection is above and beyond any other life experience (remember our ecstatic HMP subjects, Rebecca and Don, in Chapter 2?) The fact that the euphoric brain lights up like a Christmas tree when gazing on a new love may bring us closer to explaining, at least in neurological terms, why "love is blind."

So, despite all the hope and excitement associated with new love, we still need to enter into our HMPs consciously, with open eyes and feet squarely planted on the ground.

BRAINY FINDINGS

Italian researchers, Donatella Marazziti and G.B. Cassano, state: "different triggers, such as hormonal changes, life events, age, etc., may change our brain chemistry or functioning. Such changes can predispose our brain to become susceptible to stimuli coming from another person, and ultimately, to fall in love."

It's true that our brain chemistry and attachment habits may change during the passing years, with hearts-and-flowers romance sometimes taking a back seat to the more practical, day-to-day routines of life.

Still, there's no question that the biological drive to connect and create meaningful love attachments is essential for us to understand, if we truly want fulfilling and lasting partnerships.

SUMMING IT UP

In this chapter, I've presented a few facts, theories and research related to brain chemistry and how it affects lust, attraction and attachment.

I've also touched on the biological and evolutionary aspects of human attraction, as well as how we are chemically predisposed to falling in love as we become drawn into the HMP experience.

Now, to add even more to your understanding of the HMP and lasting love, let's examine the more social aspects of what I call The Culture of Love.

CHAPTER 7
The Culture of Love

"Culture is the sum of all the forms of art, of love, and of thought, which, in the course of centuries, have enabled man to be less enslaved."

—Andre Malraux

"Culture is the widening of the mind and of the spirit."

—Jawaharlal Nehru

Although societies and cultures around the world encounter love in their own distinct ways, let's take a look at something that's more than an arbitrary social construct. I call it the Culture of Love.

Attraction, romance, intimacy, human connection, compatibility, the inevitable ups and downs of relationships as well as the HMP, are all parts of the Culture of Love. It's a wide-ranging social phenomenon that goes beyond mere definition, transcends geography, nationality, race and socio-economic status, and is an essential part of the human experience. The psychology behind the search for love, motivations for entering relationships, internet dating and our views on marriage, all contribute to this culture.

The HMP occupies a special place within the Culture of Love. In fact, I see the HMP as the Culture of Love's primary pathway to a long-term relationship, with enough strength to shape partnerships and, for better or for worse, impact social interactions.

But, as I mentioned earlier, the HMP is all too often looked upon by many people as trite, hormone-driven, and a futile exercise in superficiality. Some even view this first step into love as something confined to the romantic fantasies of Hollywood movies, as opposed to being an essential part of our Culture of Love.

So, what does all this mean to you, on your search for successful long-term relationship?

When you understand the Culture of Love, then you can better grasp the true nature of the HMP and how it works. This knowledge will then allow you to be more effective in taking on new love—not just as some quick-fix, ephemeral experience, but as a useful and necessary tool, that critical stepping stone to enduring love.

The HMP has pull!

THE NASCENT STATE

The Italian sociologist, Francesco Alberoni, in his book *Falling in Love*, believes that in the Western world we are attracted by the dream of what he calls the "nascent state", or *statu nascenti.* Here, an individual becomes capable of joining with another to create a new and distinctive unity of heightened solidarity. In the nascent state, we're drawn to newness, as we come out of the darkness and move into the light of something truly unifying and unique – like new love. In fact, our Western tradition has always embraced the possibility for renaissance and renewal.

Fulfilling love relationships continually feature and are embodied by new beginnings. The pristine newness of being in love with one special individual has the power to make life extraordinary. It's that natural pull toward freshness, originality, and connection with another that drives us to search for intimacy beyond the self. So, naturally, we continue to search for the "relationship of our dreams," that singular connection that we can return to time and time again.

But it's not as simple as all that, because the search for love is informed by society's own powerful pull—this through various influences, customs and mores, all of which affect the way we think and act.

CULTURAL CONDITIONING—THE CULPRIT

Without being consciously aware of it, we routinely assume that how we feel and act should conform to what we take in from those around us. This includes the seductive daily drone of the media, with all its manipulations and cultural myths. So much of how we feel about prescribed standards of beauty and everything related to love is learned through this socio-cultural barrage of information.

We've all been bombarded by commercials relentlessly pushing designer clothes, high-priced makeup, perfumes, colognes, trendy workouts, weight loss schemes. All of them guarantee to make you irresistible—the perfect catch.

And the ad spin doesn't stop there. It goes on *ad nauseum* to define what a perfect relationship is supposed look like.

One of the reasons that we're so susceptible to suggestive advertising is our brain's tendency to form foundations on which we make future decisions. As we're growing up, we develop certain preferences based on our responses to people and experiences in our lives. Psychologists believe that by our teenage years, this develops into a kind of "love map," a personal list of likes and dislikes that dictates how we are *supposed* to feel and behave. So by sophomore year in high school, our contact with various people in our lives, as well as popular media sources, gives us a prescribed picture of what we're supposed to be looking for in a partner and how to go about "acquiring" them.

Then, when the magic moment of meeting happens, our minds and bodies ignite our expectations, not only with a firestorm of neurochemicals released by the brain (as we learned in the previous chapter), but also with a slew of conditioned influences and beliefs.

I don't know about you, but I'm against anyone telling me who I'm supposed to like or how I'm supposed to search for love. I have the right and the freedom to choose, not based on some cookie-cutter cultural directive!

The couples I've interviewed expressed similar sentiments when asked why they chose to seek out love as opposed to living a more unobtrusive single life. Surprisingly, many of my interviewees commented that they weren't even aware of their motivational processes until I asked them. But, one thing was for sure; they all wanted freedom to choose a partner without feeling like they were being manipulated by any outside source.

When we do discover that the Culture of Love's psychological drivers are often unconscious, it can help us become more aware of our true intentions so we can mindfully experience the nascent state and embark, unimpeded, on our own particular path to finding and keeping love.

INTERNET DATING—PROS AND CON ARTISTS

There are plenty of avenues in which to search for human connection, and internet dating has become more and more central to our Culture of Love. It's an exploding, billion-dollar-a-year business, as evidenced by the slew of online dating sites available to singles today.

This ever-expanding social phenomenon has been proven and well documented to be a viable way for individuals to meet, regardless of geographic location. Are you a horse lover? Into kinky fetishes? Archeological digs? Hooking up? There's something for everyone, with new specialty sites popping up all the time.

Internet dating and its increasing popularity is a testament to the enormous draw that we all have toward love, companionship, and human connection. Online dating, with all its computerized advantages and disadvantages, goes hand-in-hand with the HMP.

On the positive side, internet dating provides a way to meet that "special someone" with greater ease from the relative safety of one's home. At the same time, social media sites like Facebook and Twitter are also making it easier to communicate with a prospective love interest without the initial tension and fear sometimes associated with connecting in person.

The ease of e-dating can offer a jumpstart and the self-empowerment we need when searching for new love, especially if we're somewhat shy, introverted, or have recently ended a relationship. Remember, we're social creatures, wired for connection. Reaching out to new people in this way can be so satisfying and ultimately rewarding.

Elizabeth, one of my delightful interviewees, weighs in with some positive aspects of online dating:

"I like it that you already have a lot of personal information as opposed to blindly meeting someone at a party or a bar...If the guy writes that he doesn't want kids, and I do, then I can just move on to the next one."

Nevertheless, online dating isn't always a simple walk in the virtual park—it does have its drawbacks.

It's no secret that there are lots of psychological games being played online by men and women who unfortunately prey upon, deceive, and are quick to judge or mislead the other. This is where online dating can turn into a hollow, heavily controlled game of deception, where people may be regarded as easily manipulated, two-dimensional commodities on the cyberspace meat market.

Then there're the HMP junkies who go for the biochemical high, the quick sex fix, a la online hook-up sites created for those who have little interest in anything like long-term intimacy. These are the ones who typically seek and engage in HMP's, one after the other, yet never move beyond initial attraction, avoiding anything approaching the Commitment Stage.

In addition, the world of computer dating is literally riddled with gender stereotypes, which only end up confusing and misleading those who sincerely seek to love and be loved (if this paragraph sparks your interest, you'll definitely like the next chapter!).

Generally speaking, and I do mean generally, I've found that men tend to seek out physical attractiveness more than women and are more concerned with the age and "youngness" of their match. Women are more likely to base their responses on a man's occupation, social status, and moneymaking ability.

To illicit a positive online response, men are more likely to offer financial security and status, while women are more likely to highlight their physical attractiveness. And how about those out-of-date profile pictures? He said he was *how young?*

Researcher Elaine Hatfield appears to back up my observations with her own socio-cultural perspective:

"In evolutionary terms, men should prefer mates who possess traits signaling their reproductive value—traits such as youth and good looks—whereas women should prefer men who possess traits that signal their potential for resource acquisition—men who are able and willing to provide resources."

Although I'm aware of these particular motivational differences, I believe that online love shouldn't be driven by mere concerns with a man's bank account or with a woman's sex appeal. We're much more complex than that.

Nevertheless, with online dating, we do tend to attract people at the same level of mental healthiness (or unhealthiness) as ourselves. There's always a reason why we attract who we attract.

As my interviewee, Elizabeth, puts it:

"With online dating, you get what you're ready for, a la the 'Law of Attraction.' You learn the lessons you need to learn. It's all reflected back at you. If you have a pattern of meeting abusive people, then you will attract them wherever you are, online or not."

I see internet dating as an open invitation to the HMP. But even if you get that invitation, it's up to you to "RSVP" and to eventually connect "in the flesh." After all, if you never actually met and your communication is limited to an endless series of back-and-forth emails, there's no place to go with a promising love relationship—nothing will progress.

Then again, you might come to realize that this way of dating just isn't for you. Not everyone responds favorably to all the hype and marketing gimmicks associated with online dating. Meeting another person the old-fashioned way, at a local party or a singles meet-up group, may be a more appealing and natural way to connect—it's your call. In any event, I feel that entering a relationship with a new partner mustn't be wholly replaced by or limited to the streamlined, technological and potentially abbreviated experience of internet dating.

But if you do choose to enter into the mysterious waters of dating sites, I urge you to keep things in perspective and always stay computer-safe. With that said, online dating can definitely be a legitimate and useful tool (perhaps an art?) for personal and social exploration.

WHY WE SEARCH—FIVE FACTORS

Within the Culture of Love, there are several motivating factors that inspire us to search for love. Here's my top five, with a brief explanation for each of these factors in order to show the close relationship between the HMP and the Culture of Love:

1. **Anticipation and excitement of the HMP.**
The excitement and imminent romance of the HMP often gives way to the anticipation of long-term possibilities such as intimate partnership, marriage and family. Many of my research subjects reported that, at the beginning of the HMP, they felt a strong sense of excitement, sometimes for no particular reason (here's that unconscious human desire for newness and connection that I spoke of earlier). It's this excitement and anticipation that typically energizes the HMP.

2. **Opportunity for personal growth and inspiration.**
The HMP experience can be a real opportunity to apply self-knowledge and take your "self-growth show" on the road. Many individuals reported that being committed to their partner helped them gain a sense of personal responsibility. Such dedication can be incredibly inspiring, and a rekindling of inspiration and creativity is just what we need to maintain the momentum of the HMP.

3. **Attainment of higher status and acceptance in society.**
New love relationships often lead to higher status and legitimacy in the eyes of mainstream society. Despite the positive image and attention given to bachelors and free-spirit types, couples are often more validated and legitimized by mainstream culture. Is it any wonder that a large portion of advertising is targeted toward couples? Many of my interviewees claimed that social acceptance was their motivation for starting a love relationship. After all, as we grow older, we don't want to be seen as "old maids," "cougars," or as "wolves on the prowl." Clearly, people's motivations to avoid stigma and feel accepted by their culture are natural, powerful and understandable.

4. **Relief of escaping the single life.**
This motivating factor is closely related to the desire for higher social status and acceptance. Many see their newfound partner as a ticket out of the lonely single scene. Wanting to escape single life is certainly understandable, but in order for the HMP to be successful, couples must transcend this prevailing perspective. They will do well to see their relationship as something intrinsically vital and infused with great meaning, not just as a means to an end.

5. **Benefits of well-being and longer life.**
Fulfilling our inherent desire for newness and companionship is not only mentally and spiritually nurturing, but also has been shown to improve physical health. It's now known that married men tend to live longer. Even the prospect of marriage may contribute to better health, perhaps because the responsibility to stand beside one's part-

ner can be incredibly empowering.

TAKING NOTE OF MARRIAGE

Lifelong love connections are often the end goal of "the search," which is why marriage is front-and-center in the Culture of Love. The best marriages are not those built upon rules, fear of abandonment, not wanting to be alone or unrealistic expectations, but rather those based on love and shared happiness. It's about two people working to create something greater than themselves through love, commitment and mutual understanding.

Not every HMP eventually takes the form of a conventional marriage. However, the natural outcome of a successful HMP will be a life-long partnership in one form or another.

Unfortunately, you don't have to look far to find people supremely dissatisfied with their marriages, which may last decades upon terrible decades – the exact opposite of a Honeymoon Forever!

Who hasn't heard horror stories or read about the latest divorce statistics? The saddest part about failed marriages is that most of them probably started off as perfectly satisfying, healthy HMP's. So, what happened?

I believe that individuals can build dynamic, happy relationships if they're willing to put in the effort it takes to continuously renew the original power of the HMP. It takes sustained motivation and recommitment to something bigger. Marriage vows are not just for the wedding day!

A CULTURED SUMMARY

Whether through a better understanding of certain culturally motivating factors or through the modern wonder of online dating, you've now been provided with some general knowledge related to the Culture of Love. This is knowledge you don't want to overlook, and I hope it will assist you on your way to eventual love success.

I want you to succeed in love!

CHAPTER 8
Men and Women are from Planet Earth

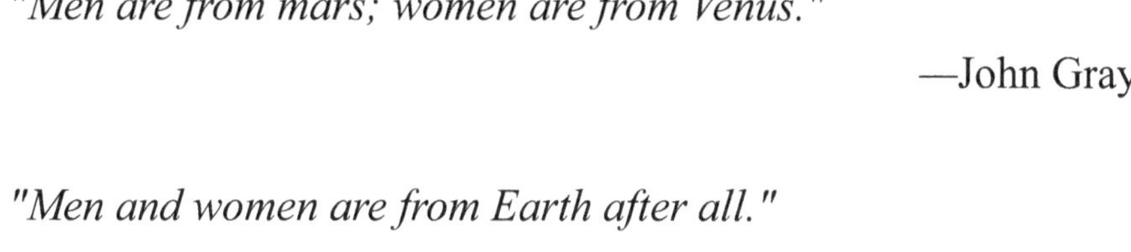

"Men are from mars; women are from Venus."

—John Gray

"Men and women are from Earth after all."

—John Bradshaw

We're about to enter the perplexing and controversial world of gender. It can be quite challenging, but understanding gender is critical when forging an enduring connection with your partner.

The initial joining of men and women has long been viewed from a flawed, often divisive point of view. That's why gender stereotypes should always be considered while in a relationship, since there's always a mustard seed of truth contained within them. They must also be mindfully scrutinized in order to see how an optimal HMP experience and ever-developing relationship can bring the sexes together in a way that unifies rather than divides.

The mother (and father) of all gender stereotypes seems to be that men and women are completely different from one another, two disparate sexes hopelessly divided by the circumstances of biology. I don't subscribe to this brand of worn-out thinking and want to challenge it here and now.

The truth is that men and women are not as different from one another as most stereotypes would have us believe. Some gender differences need to be acknowledged, but never allowed to act as wedges that drive people into lonely corners. Instead, I want you to see these stereotypes for what they really are, what they represent and how they affect you.

Often, these gender stereotypes are harmful and constitute a highly negative way of looking at our world that certainly won't lead to empowering HMP's or any lasting relationships. Stereotypical thinking is, by definition, gender discrimination. It's ultimately divisive, and has no place in this book or anywhere on the planet.

Two sexes divided cannot stand!

GENDER STEREOTYPES

Gender stereotypes thrive in a climate of extremes and black-and-white thinking. These stereotypes are gross generalizations that can, at best, vaguely resemble the general nature of men and women. And Lord knows, we can't base our lives on generalizations, because life is lived one action, one moment, one person at a time, each with its own particular bent. This in-the-moment style of living needs to be a part of any fulfilled life, let alone any meaningful love relationship.

If we learn to balance this spontaneity with mindful focus and a more discerning viewpoint regarding men and women, we can create and sustain the best of life-long relationships and have HMP's that last forever.

I'd be wrong if I didn't take a moment to present some of these intriguing yet flawed stereotypes, which unfortunately remain firmly entrenched in the collective consciousness of Western culture.

Here's a chart that lists some of these gender stereotypes, stemming from the supposed differences between men and women, along with some corresponding comments:

THOSE DAMNED GENDER STEREOTYPES!

Men:	**Women:**
Only think about sexual conquest	Only seek deeper emotional connection
Pursue and control women	Wait to be pursued and passively submit to men
Want to fix problems rather than listening to their partners	Would rather have their partners fix their problems as opposed to just hearing their problems
Are stupid	Are schemers
Are only mechanically-minded and into sports	Are not mechanically-minded and are not into sports
Are prowlers	Are home-bodies
Are self-centered	Are selfless nurturers
Are disconnected from their feelings	Are irrational and overly connected to their feelings

CONQUEST AND CONNECTION

Many people tend to associate typical male courtship habits with possessiveness, control, and even animal-like hunting behavior. Men supposedly leave their scent everywhere and continuously display their bravado in an attempt to chase and capture their feminine prey. One interviewee of ours even exclaimed, "Men are so primal! They sow their seed all over the place!"

These actions seem to portray men as sex-crazed beasts only concerned with the forceful acquisition of an unassuming mate. Such a view leaves no room for the very real treasures that lie beneath that surface of pure physicality.

If we look deeper into this masculine stereotype, there are complexities to be considered and questions to be answered. For example, why do men initiate the chase? They often do so because they like to create a dramatic backdrop for the relationship they're pursuing. They search out "damsels in distress" in order to become "knights in shining armor."

This inclination actually reveals the innate desire that men have for intimate relationships. They want relationships that go beyond sexual gratification. They want it to be romantic and ideal. Men often have different ways of demonstrating this, but the underlying longing for connection is the same.

Conversely, some believe that women tend to withhold sex, and instead prefer a more substantive emotional connection. While it's true that many women desire emotional intimacy, this does not mean they aren't sexual beings. They just prefer sex to be built on a foundation of love and often do not want to be participants in empty lust.

As you can see, both the male quest for sex and the female quest for emotional intimacy can lead to the same place—meaningful long-term partnership.

THE HUNTER AND THE HUNTED

The gender stereotype of "pursuer vs. pursued" or "controlling vs. passive" is closely connected to the notion of male conquest. This belief portrays men as tyrannical tribal leaders who only wish to control or manipulate.

Historically, men have used their protective yet pursuing instincts to be in control of most situations. Even though this masculine bent towards power, control and leadership does exist, it can be seen as something positive and beneficial. Most men are well-suited and happy to lead, serving as the definitive defenders of their partners.

Conversely, women have customarily been seen as gentler and more nurturing, yet more passive. This perceived passivity shouldn't necessarily be seen as something entirely negative. We could all use relationships with more gentleness and less aggression.

I acknowledge the importance of *both* partners stepping up and taking an equal and active role in the nurturing of their relationship. Any healthy HMP must be co-created and helped along by each member of the couple. Building a relationship should never be a matter of one person controlling or coercing the other, or either person submissively waiting to have love handed to them on a silver platter—it takes two.

THE HEAD AND THE HEART

This particular stereotype depicts men as coldly analytical brutes who seem uninterested in the inevitable trials and tribulations of their partner. They just want to control the situation, handling problems with a "confront and solve" mentality rather than empathically listening to their female counterparts.

As I mentioned, I don't deny that men may have controlling tendencies. Men often think that they're genuinely being helpful by making the decisions and tying to solve all their partner's problems. I'd like to acknowledge again that this tendency can sometimes be positive and not just a driving need to govern or to "run the show."

Conversely, when facing problems, it appears that most women want more compassion and understanding from their partners. Women routinely share with me their hope that men will resist the urge to see problems as situations that can only be examined from a cold and calculating perspective. They want their men to communicate from a place of warmth, understanding, and empathy. And isn't this what true intimacy is all about?

And all this requires personal involvement, for true empathy comes only from experiencing and identifying with what your partner is going through. It's not difficult to see why the close connection that this kind of understanding creates is so desirable to women. But don't men want this kind of intimate connection, too?

Once again, even though the actions of men and women may appear different, they both share a common underlying desire, not only to be listened to and understood, but for enduring connection, as well.

NEANDERTHALS AND WITCHES

There's a particularly destructive cultural stereotype going around, which holds that men are stupid and unable to act with any intelligence. This stereotype also suggests that women are able to overpower the simple brutishness of men with their superior, scheming intelligence. Hence all those demeaning "dumb husband" T.V. commercials and sitcoms where men's endless stupidity and clumsiness are the name of the game.

The truth of the matter is that men do tend to think and act in a more linear, black-and-white fashion than women, whose multi-tasking thoughts and actions can be misunderstood by men as controlling and intimidating. Both the alleged stupidity of men and deviousness of women are often products of the worst kind of stereotypical thinking—real killers of any promising partnership.

There's nothing inherently wrong with the way that either gender thinks and acts. Linear and intuitive thinking certainly have their place, and multi-tasking can be useful and something to admire. Still, these assigned gender differences routinely cause problems, especially when it leads to gross misunderstandings or uninformed judgments.

FOOTBALL AND SHOPPING

Have you heard the stereotype about men only being interested in fixing stuff or parking their lazy butts on the couch to watch Sunday football? After all, what else is there in life for guys besides *Popular Mechanics* and *Sports Illustrated: The Swimsuit Edition*?

For this is traditionally the sanctified realm of testosterone.

And we all know that women can't repair anything by themselves, and they certainly couldn't care less about anything connected to the masculine glory of the sporting world, let alone "the thrill of victory, and the agony of defeat."

Wrong! It turns out that both men and women love sports. Women can be perfectly capable when it comes to home repairs (after all, not every man out there is a master builder). And, contrary to popular belief, men do watch reruns of "Friends" and actually enjoy it.

So be careful about initial judgments and assumptions when it comes to your partner's skills and interests. You might just find that you have more in common than you originally thought. Successful relationships go much deeper than gender stereotypes about football games or fashion runways.

SKIRT-CHASERS AND HOMEMAKERS

Then there are all those wily, sneaky men who prowl the city looking for unsuspecting, docile female homebodies who sit at home baking sugar cookies. "Men only want one thing…" is the stereotypical line thrown out about womanizers and sexual predators, although hardly fair to most men. Sure, men are capable of this kind of negative behavior and they often pay dearly for it. But time and again, their search for sex stems not so much from the need to dominate, but from a basic desire for intimacy and nurturance.

In the same way, the "homebody" stereotype that women have gotten stuck with—such as, "A woman's place is in the kitchen!"—is yet another snarky expression describing what is actually a display of love, commitment, and security for many women. The focus needs to be more on the underlying desire for lasting companionship that men and women share, rather than on the stereotype itself, which can really damage the new bond forged during the HMP.

TAKERS AND GIVERS

How about the stereotype that men are self-centered cads who only care about themselves and what they can get from others? Take, take, take is that endless and selfish battle cry of all those guys whose only goal is to rip-off others and satisfy themselves. And, of course, there are those selfless, hopelessly codependent women-folk, the devoted ones, always at the ready to serve their men. They're the selfless nurturers whose only reason to live is to give, never thinking about their own basic needs and wants. "Stand by your man”—no matter what!

In reality, any man or woman can be a taker or a giver, depending on the circumstances. In fact, learning to be both a giver and a taker is a noble goal for anyone embarking on a journey into love. It requires each partner to foster respect for one another through a workable balance of a healthy give and take, humility and pride, selfishness and selflessness.

HARD ASSES AND CRY BABIES

Oh, those unfeeling men, those hopeless, heartless creatures, completely cut-off from their emotions. And all those over-the-top, irrational women who just hysterically react to everything under the sun. Sigmund Freud started this stereotype with his patriarchal notions of over-emotional, histrionic women.

It's no secret that everybody's got feelings, though some have more trouble than others appropriately expressing and connecting to them. Still, strong men cry, and women can coolly reason things out about as good as anybody.

The thing to remember is that a healthy inner emotional life consists of both free expression and logical reasoning, a la Mr. Spock, no matter the gender. And a healthy relationship is no different. Partners need to be mindful of one another to ensure that both sides of the emotional spectrum are given space to be expressed without undue judgment or ego-centered patronization.

PROBLEMS AND SOLUTIONS

Now that we've taken some time to highlight a few of the more common gender stereotypes, it should be easier to shed the belief that men and women will never be able to understand each other. It's this misunderstanding that all too often stifles the passion and excitement of the HMP, thereby crushing the positive momentum of hopeful love and commitment.

In order for new couples to tap into the full potential of the HMP, a mutual and open expression of their needs and wants is optimal. Hopefully, they'll also have the desire to commit to the time it takes to get to know each another, not through the myopic lens of gender stereotypes, but through the spirit of rigorous honesty and radical acceptance.

Here's what two of our interviewees had to say:

Clement: "I just want to be validated as the kind of man I really am, not what society says I'm supposed to be. I want to hear that I'm a strong person with integrity and good character, not judged by some stupid stereotype."

Luci:"I want acceptance of who I am. Please don't try to change me into who you think I should be. I get so tired of men seeing me as just another 'typical' woman. I want them to accept me exactly as I am, not as some stereotypical fantasy."

Some powerful and eye-opening statements, don't you think?

COMING TOGETHER—A FINAL THOUGHT

At their deepest levels, both men and women resonate with the same core values of love, family, trust, security and caring.

The HMP is the perfect time to free yourself from the negative influence of generalized stereotypes. It's a great opportunity to allow yourself to see gender differences as complementary rather than as excuses or exclusionary beliefs that can sabotage a relationship before it has a chance to begin. It's always best to learn about your new partner's behaviors so that you can create a complementary balance with each other, right from the beginning.

The necessity for unifying the male and female genders extends beyond love relationships, as well. In recent decades, the institution of patriarchy and everything associated with it has finally come under well-deserved fire. Even though patriarchal thinking still exists, it's time to finally move out of a male dominated age into a more harmonious one—where men and women are equal and work together, not in spite of their differing traits, but because of them.

History shows us that any attempt to focus solely on male or female energy results in a subversion of the two genders, where the strength of each become tragically sapped or needlessly diluted. True collaboration lies in the unification of masculine and feminine energies. We need both the warrior spirit of men and the nurturing power of women.

I think this is happening, but slowly.

CHAPTER 9
Co-Conspirators—Addiction, Shame & Self-sabotage

"My beloved angel, I am nearly mad about you, as much as one can be mad. I can no longer think of anything but you. I grasp you, I kiss you, I caress you, a thousand of the most amorous caresses take possession of me. But my God, what is to become of me, if you have deprived me of my reason?"

—Honore de Balzac to Eveline Hanska (1835)

"Your task is not to seek for love, but merely to seek and find all the barriers within yourself that you have built against it."

—Rumi

Up until now, there's been a lot of positive talk about the HMP and its relationship to blossoming love, but I don't want to sugar-coat it. And I wouldn't be of good service to you if I didn't alert you to some of the darker corners of the human condition that can stop any new love dead in its tracks.

Enter with me now into the seamy underworld of addiction, shame and self-sabotage, so that you can avoid tumbling into the sticky traps that'll surely destroy any promising love relationship.

PROGRAMMED FOR CONNECTION

We humans are programmed for connection. We're social animals, and we need secure attachments. That connection is usually a good thing, until it lapses into the area of that obsessive-compulsive behavior that John Bowlby, the renowned Twentieth Century social psychologist, called the "Attachment Crisis." In fact, he believed that problems such as addiction came from one's basic inability to connect with another person.

If we don't learn how to truly connect in healthy, fulfilling ways, then the opportunity for true intimacy becomes squelched and addictions can easily emerge.

ADDICTION AND DEFINITIONS

While addiction takes many forms for those who fall into its shadowy depths, many have a pretty good idea of what it looks like and the wreckage it leaves in its wake.

Most of us mental health professionals have come to know all too well the many faces of addiction, either through work in the field or from our own personal life experiences. One thing we've learned is that addiction crosses all boundaries of gender, culture, politics, religion and socio-economic status—no one is immune.

Many definitions of addiction have been bandied about over time, but the one I like best is this one:

Addiction is any pathological relationship with a mind-altering substance or behavior that has life-damaging consequences.

This definition includes any unhealthy alliance that can throw a person into an extremely skewed, unbalanced way of being. It almost always includes fantasy, shame and self-sabotaging behavior.

Here's another definition of addiction, straight from a recovering addict:

"Addiction is the use of a substance or activity, for the purpose of lessening pain or augmenting pleasure by a person who has lost control over the rate, frequency, or duration of its use, and whose life has become progressively unmanageable as a result."

I'd like to add:

Addiction is an unhealthy and ultimately unworkable way to avoid reality and self-medicate, in an attempt to lessen the pain of life's day-to-day problems and challenges.

Behaviors become addictions when there is a loss of control or when an individual can't stop a certain behavior, therefore resulting in pain, life chaos, and even death. No matter what particular form an addiction takes, one thing is for sure: the underlying causes and basic mechanisms of all addictions are essentially the same.

LOVE ADDICTION

Just as there is addiction to drugs and alcohol, there is the lesser-known malady of Love Addiction. Actually, this addiction isn't about love at all. And it certainly doesn't have anything to do with love success.

Rather, Love Addiction is about the desperation to escape loneliness, which ironically enough leads one to even more social isolation and that sinking feeling of disconnection. This addiction may also manifest as a frantic clinging to another person or the pressing need to withdraw.

World lecturer and former psychotherapist, Anne Wilson Schaef, calls this kind of behavior (and the title of her book) an "escape from intimacy." In a relationship overshadowed by addiction, there's no sense of the personal integrity or strength that normally accompanies two people in a healthy partnership. Instead, intense drama, possessiveness, mental obsession and compulsive behavior become par for the course.

LOVE ADDICTED BEHAVIOR

Love addicted behavior is all about the need for a fix, not unlike the self-defeating ways of any drug addict or alcoholic. Addicts will anxiously look outside themselves for a sense of empowerment, rather than looking inward where true integrity and self-love are really found.

Paradoxically, though the love addict can often seem clingy, obsessive and almost hypnotically drawn to their so-called beloved, their dysfunctional behavior actually stems from just the opposite—

an enormous fear of closeness.

This often unconscious, obsessive drive to own or even "take the other hostage" is, at the end of the day, an expression of their own inner disconnectedness. We call this outward drive for inner healing Codependence.

The addicted lover then becomes almost narcissistic, with insatiable infatuation feeding only the most selfish of desires. He or she fabricates what they want their lover to be rather than allowing them to be who they really are.

When the relationship ends, as it usually does, one or both individuals may experience sharp feelings of rejection, anger, depression, fear or anxiety. Sometimes, these turbulent emotions may lead to stalking, or even worse, homicide and suicide.

Love Addiction's inevitable, tragic fall-out includes the prospect of love remaining forever foreign, alienating and ultimately unobtainable – again, the exact opposite of a Honeymoon Forever.

THE ROOTS OF ADDICTIVE LOVE

Addictive love has been with us for a long time and is usually rooted in our childhoods. As children, we attempted to keep our parents or other caregivers around. We learned that our very survival depended on them caring for us. If they weren't there, we had to fend for ourselves, often in very unhealthy ways though we did our best. It's a safe bet to say that most of these early needs and wants were never adequately met.

As we enter adulthood we continue our attempt, often unconsciously, to get thcsc basic dependency needs met—things like touch and attention, thinking that we'll self-destruct if they don't materialize. It's when we attempt to start a love relationship with this kind of immature, though well-intentioned, thinking or survival mentality that can spell trouble and possible disaster between non-suspecting partners. Most relationships do contain some degree of addictiveness and dependency even as we attempt to seek out that healthier, give-and-take state of *inter*dependency.

Now, if these early developmental needs aren't met, then who we choose as potential partners will be highly suspect and potentially catastrophic, not only to our well-being but to our very existence. We can't see the other person clearly for who they really are, and we blindly act out impulsively because of what we didn't receive earlier in life.

This over-reliance on and obsessive need to control our partner, in order to distract from our current fears and inner pain, often becomes the basis for addictive love. This highly destructive behavior then turns into a desperate quest for balance and self-acceptance through an outside source, often through another person.

Along with these self-defeating behaviors come those awful feelings of toxic shame and self-deprecating beliefs, such as:

- "I'm a loser."

- "I'm unlovable."

- "I'm worthless."

- "I'll never get what I want."

- "I don't deserve love."

- "If they really knew the truth about me, they'd leave."

As these self-blaming beliefs progress, we end up not getting what we want or need, especially from a prospective partner. In fact, we become even more controlling, needy, self-hating, unstable, self-destructive and hopelessly shame-based. We never grow up and certainly become less attractive or available for any healthy love relationship. Honeymoon Phases can never thrive in this kind of self-sabotaging and emotionally poisonous atmosphere.

To someone like a love addict, even a pathological relationship may seem normal. Ironically, the unhealthiness may feel almost comfortable because it's so familiar, a known quantity. The addict exclaims, "What's a relationship without the drama and the abuse? It's all I've ever known!"

THE LOVE ADDICT AND THE LOVE AVOIDANT

Pia Mellody, Senior Clinical Advisor to The Meadows, a world-renowned addiction treatment center, is one of the top experts on Love Addiction.

In her groundbreaking book, *Facing Love Addiction*, she writes extensively about co-addicted relationships and discusses this paradox of outward obsession and inward disconnectedness.

Mellody describes one partner as the "Love Addict" and the

other partner as the "Love Avoidant." She states, "Just as the Love Addict clings and displays neediness for the other, the Love Avoidant displays an opposite trait, a distancing or self-alienation from desire."

This particular characterization of unhealthy lovers by Mellody is as insightful as it is impressive:

> *The addictive priority for a Love Addict is the partner and the fantasy the Love Addict has developed about that partner. Love Addicts are obsessed with the partner and seek to create intensity inside the relationship—actually to the point of enmeshment rather than establishing healthy intimacy. Love Avoidants are interested in creating intensity outside the relationship. Any other addiction will do the job of causing a Love Avoidant to evade intimacy within the relationship by focusing on the outside addiction.*

Notice that the Love Addict and the Love Avoidant share the same addictive tendencies. They seem to be opposites; one wants love, while the other avoids it, but in reality, they both desire closeness and don't know how to achieve it. So they usually resort to suffocating closeness or running away from their partners, hardly healthy ways to lasting connection.

OTHER PERSPECTIVES ON ADDICTIVE LOVE

Addictive lovers labor under the illusion that the dependent relationship will heal their pain and ease their fears. The challenge we face is to identify and acknowledge addictive elements and do what we can to change them.

Here are twenty prominent characteristics of addictive love as listed by Brenda Schaffer in her book, *Signs of Addictive Love*. I've added my own interpretations of how these symptoms are typically expressed in italics.

The person in an addicted relationship:

• Feels consumed: *"I can't think about anything or anybody else!"*

• Cannot define ego boundaries: *"I call him thirty times a day!"*

• Exhibits sadomasochism: *"Oh, the pain! This must be love!"*

• Fears letting go: *"I can never really relax in this relationship. He might leave me..."*

• Fears risk, change and the unknown: *"What if I get hurt? What if things change? What if, what it, what if?"*

• Allows little individual growth: *"She doesn't give me any space!"*

• Lacks true intimacy: *"I love him because I need him."*

• Plays psychological games: *"I've got it all under control. I can read her like a book."*

• Gives in order to get: *"If I give her enough stuff, then she'll give me everything I need, including sex."*

• Attempts to change the other: *"I know what I'll do! I'll get him to get rid of that awful laugh of his!"*

• Needs the other to feel complete: *"If I didn't have her, I couldn't exist!"*

• Seeks solutions outside the self: *"When we're finally married, I'll finally be happy."*

• Demands and expects to be the sole receiver of love: *"You'll always love me, and nobody else, right?"*

• Refuses commitment: *"I like you, but I don't know if I love you. Let's just see how it goes."*

• Looks to the other for affirmation and self-worth, over and over, day after day: *"Do you think I'm okay? Am I good enough? Do you like my hat?"*

•Fears abandonment upon routine separation: *"Where are you going? To the market? Don't leave me!"*

• Re-creates old negative feelings: *"You're just like my ex! See, I knew I couldn't trust you!"*

• Desires, yet fears, closeness: *"Not tonight, dear, I have a headache...again."*

• Attempts to take care of their partner in a way that strips them of their identity, their whole being: *"With me in your life, you'll never have to think about anything!"*

• Plays power games: *"You'll never make it out there without me. I'm the real brains in this outfit!"*

THE SHAME OF IT ALL

This may be a hard truth, but so many of us just don't think much of ourselves. In fact, too often we're ashamed, as if we don't measure up and don't deserve the good things in life—especially love.

The real underlying cause of addictive behaviors is toxic shame, which is almost always hatched early in life and then carried into adulthood. All addictive behaviors stem from shame, including that awful sense of low self-esteem and feelings of defectiveness and worthlessness. Shame can have us falsely believing that we're damaged goods, that we don't measure up, that we're just not good enough.

John Bradshaw in his first book, *Healing the Shame That Binds You*, writes extensively about the concept of "toxic shame" and the damage it causes to our souls, our very being:

"To have shame as an identity is to believe that one's being is flawed, that one is defective as a human being. Once shame is transformed into an identity, it becomes toxic and dehumanizing."

I could write volumes about the origins and harmful effects of shame. But suffice to say, when we're shame-based we just don't think enough of ourselves to make self-care a priority. We stay stuck in our own muck, wallowing in immaturity and, too often, in the turbulent wake of addiction.

Remember, we tend to attract people who are at the same level of psychological health or unhealthiness as we are. So, if we've done the required work on ourselves and have achieved a degree of mental health, we're likely to meet someone just like us—someone who's physically, spiritually, and emotionally available.

CULTIVATING HEALTHY LOVE

If you do find you or your partner sinking into addictive behaviors, it's critical that you find support to stop the destructive behavior and come to terms with what a healthy relationship is really all about.

If you have addictive tendencies, you'll need to gain a better understanding of the particular destructive ways in which you interact with others. With the support of safe and reliable helpers, most addictions can lose their powerful grip. Taking the time to care for yourself in this way will allow you to bring a fuller and more complete self to your relationship, which will ultimately help both you and your partner to grow in love.

Sadly, the HMP can be a hiding place for those who can't or won't make a commitment. They don't want to make the transition from the passion-filled HMP into something truly sustainable. In fact, many people would rather embark on a continuous cycle of HMPs. They go round and round the HMP cycle, like an endless ride on a carousel to nowhere, never achieving true intimacy or long-term commitment.

What these phobic types may not realize is that the newness of love, like the nascent state, can actually coexist and grow into a fulfilling long-term commitment to one partner. Unfortunately, these individuals never get very far, never really tap into the HMP's built-in possibility for lifelong love. Instead, they're always finding themselves at the very beginning, treading water in the shallow end of intimacy, which is really no intimacy at all.

I believe that the challenge of seeking lasting love is worth the risk of going beyond the initial HMP and into the more uncharted and ultimately more rewarding waters of a fulfilling lasting partnership.

ACCORDING TO JOHN GRAY

Author John Gray believes that there's an inevitable point in every relationship during which we must confront our own demons:

> *[There] is a time in relationships when we experience our own unresolved pain or our shadow self. It is when our lid comes off and our painful feelings emerge. It is a time of solitary growth when we need to look more to ourselves*

than to our partners for love and fulfillment. It is a time of healing. This is the time when men hibernate in their caves and women sink to the bottom of their wells.

The point here is that a relationship will continually challenge you to improve yourself by facing the issues that make you who you are, even if the process is a painful or lonely one. Now, this meeting with the "shadow self" or our "dark side" doesn't necessarily mean that you're a love addict or love avoidant. In fact, this sort of confrontation with self is essential to personal growth and the growth of a love relationship.

DANCING WITH THE DARK SIDE

We all have our dark sides, those parts of ourselves that we're not so fond of that bring us a lot of shame. Some of us have past histories that may cause us to flirt with addiction—love and otherwise—where we end up constantly living in emotional pain and oppressive fear. Most of us, if we're not already too emotionally and spiritually damaged, would like to overcome or at least keep those more uncomplimentary parts of ourselves safely at bay.

But, how do we do that? What do we do with all this pain and suffering? Can we really ever overcome the dark side of ourselves, or are we destined to live a life of endless pain and suffering?

I believe that we need to embrace, to dance with our dark sides, and even love those less-than-flattering parts of ourselves, especially if we want healthier love relationships.

There are many avenues to deal with the dark side of self.

Some may enter into therapy. Some may join 12-Step groups and be of even greater service to others. Connecting to nature, creating art, or even changing one's diet may help to quell that shame-based way of thinking. For others, finding a spiritual practice or joining a particular religious community may be the way.

Whichever path appeals to you, all these roads can lead to a healthier and happier self through the mindful practice of self-care. Self-care is our greatest defense against addiction, toxic shame, and self-sabotage, and is the highlight of our next chapter.

CHAPTER 10
Self-care—A Love Affair

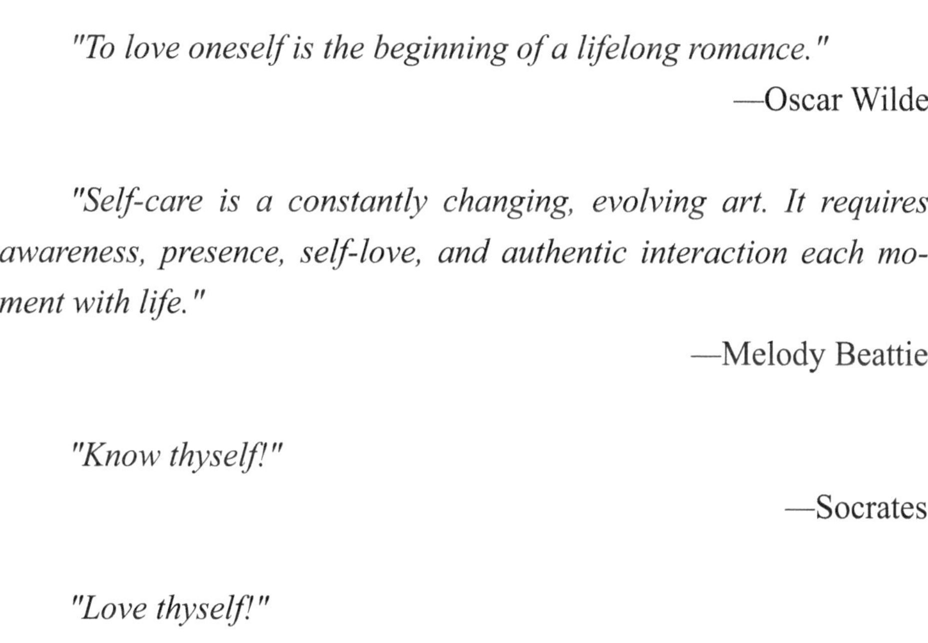

"To love oneself is the beginning of a lifelong romance."

—Oscar Wilde

"Self-care is a constantly changing, evolving art. It requires awareness, presence, self-love, and authentic interaction each moment with life."

—Melody Beattie

"Know thyself!"

—Socrates

"Love thyself!"

—Robert Page Kaufman

Many of the unpleasant elements of human interactions that I've just finished talking about stem from an unbalanced, wounded, or lost self. So, it only makes sense that a major first step to true love success is to fully take on the healing art of self-care and self-acceptance. It's the ultimate spiritual antidote to any addictive behavior and the prerequisite not only for personal growth but also for intimate connection with others.

By turning your love inward, you can come to care for yourself as much—or more—than anyone you've ever known.

You've probably heard the phrase, "Be your own best friend." How about being your own best lover, your own true soul mate? Only after you've come to love and accept yourself, including your gifts and shortcomings, can you fully love others.

By taking great care of yourself and practicing unconditional self-regard, you'll surely attract others who also treat themselves well—just the sort of people you'll love to love!

A HONEYMOON PHASE WITH SELF

In order to learn how to have a never-ending HMP, you first need to experience one internally. This soul-searching involves knowledge, understanding, and honest reflection. Again, it's really about having that love affair with yourself.

The act of loving yourself can ultimately lead to an optimum level of mental and physical health, a manageable ego, and strong protective boundaries when dealing with others. Once this is achieved, you'll not only be more open to love, you'll become a better long-term partner, too!

To be ready for love, you'll want to know who you are and what makes you tick. It will be essential to have a modicum of life fulfillment, maybe improve your communication skills, and inevitably love and care for yourself as much as you've ever loved and cared for anyone else.

When you are truly engaged in your self-imposed HMP, any relationship you enter into will be a natural outgrowth of your own self-care. When each partner learns to love and care for themselves *first*, they can experience an extraordinary bonding. And that's a great situation, the best of all possible worlds.

At the end of the day, self-care and self-acceptance are the most important prerequisites to any HMP.

SELF-CARE IN ACTION

Needless to say, there are countless ways to take care of yourself physically, psychologically, emotionally, and spiritually. To help you on your way to maximum self-care, here's my suggested list of practical ways to take better care of yourself in preparation for that wonderful love relationship you've always wanted and absolutely deserve.

EXERCISE!

Who hasn't heard this one? There's no getting around it. We all need more exercise, especially in our increasingly sedentary society.

We're hearing more and more from the media about the skyrocketing levels of obesity in Western society and its negative medical consequences: high blood pressure, heart problems, and diabetes, just to name a few.

I can't emphasize enough the importance of regular exercise if you really want to have that great love relationship. Exercise not only tones the body, but also increases energy levels and pumps up self-esteem.

Not only is exercise good for your physical well-being, but research has also shown that energizing activities such as bike riding and jogging spark passion by releasing all those feel-good pheromones. It can even make you better in the sack!

Healthy people attract healthy people. If you're not in the optimum physical shape you'd like to be in, then you'll probably attract the same. Now, in our increasingly "physical looks-oriented world," I want to state that self-care's not so much about physical appearance as it is about healthy practices. So don't obsess about whether or not your waistline is shrinking. It’s more about creating and sticking to a healthy physical routine.

If you're already exercising at the gym, practicing Yoga, Pilates, Nia, Zumba, Tai Chi or any one of the many of today's fitness options, keep up the good work. If not, start today—it's never too late.

EAT YOUR FRUITS AND VEGGIES!

Then there's the notion of a "good diet," the brass ring to health we all admire but don't always follow. Too many of us don't really eat as healthfully as we think we do.

While we're on the subject, consider these questions and see if you're paying enough attention to your particular dietary needs:

• How many of us are significantly cutting down on our consumption of dairy products and red meat?

• Are we pushing the organic fruits and veggies?

• Are we limiting our food portions and general food intake?

• Do we require something special, like a gluten-free diet?

• Are we really paying enough attention to our particular dietary needs?

Now, I'm not a dietician or a physician, and what a healthy diet is for one individual may not be for another. So, definitely check with a professional to find the best and most appropriate diet that fits you.

If you're currently taking good care of yourself with a healthy diet that fits your particular dietary needs, great. If not, as with regular exercise, it's never too late to climb aboard the "healthy food express."

All aboard!

CREATE SAFE SPACES

We all want to feel safe. It's always in our best interest to create healthy, safe spaces in our daily lives, where we can truly experience peace and serenity.

John Gray in his book, *Men Are From Mars, Women Are From Venus*, talks about men needing their own personal "man caves" to withdraw and rejuvenate. Even when involved in a prospering love relationship, both men and women need safe places to be in order to emotionally re-charge, so you can return to your new love with renewed energy.

What kinds of safe spaces are we talking about? For some, it's about creating a safe atmosphere at home, like a comforting nook or spiritual area set aside for prayer and meditation.

For others, peace of mind can be found in nature—that familiar pond, grassy meadow or enchanting pine grove. Or maybe it's a simple stroll in the salty air near the seashore or a meditative pause by a lake at sunset. It's no secret that a connection with nature provides serenity and relief from life's daily pressures and challenges.

Some people have even learned to create a safe space in their own minds through quiet moments of contemplation.

No matter where your own particular safe haven may be, it's a great way to take care of yourself.

BALANCE WORK AND PLAY

Another way to practice self-care is to develop a balanced lifestyle and a daily routine. Too many of us have crazy, skewed lifestyles. We just don't make enough time for leisure, travel, family, sleep, fun activities, spiritual pursuits—or relationships.

That brings up the problem of work. So many of us are literally killing ourselves with 100-hour work weeks. And for what? Money? Prestige? (Disease?) Have you ever wondered how so many of us were ever lured into such an overhyped and destructive "work ethic?"

The bane of "Workaholism," also called "Work Addiction," is one of the most insidious, highly addictive and ironically glorified lifestyles found in today's world. More stress-related diseases and many unhappy relationships can be attributed to this over-emphasis on work than to any other aspects of contemporary life. That's a bold statement, but it's true.

If you're working more than fifty hours a week and eating standing up, you probably won't have much time for fun and spontaneity, or possess any of the essential elements of a happy, healthy lifestyle. And you'll have a lot less time to meet others.

Do yourself a favor and find time to let loose. Unbalanced lifestyles simply don't mix with happy relationships and sane HMP's.

MAKE MONEY MATTER

Believe it or not, money matters. Volumes have been written about money—how to make it, spend it and be in right relationship to it.

According to Abraham Maslow's "Hierarchy of Needs," it's almost impossible to experience self-actualization when you're freaking out about how to pay rent or put food on the table. The struggle for funds makes it harder to survive, let alone love. So it would be wise to make sure your basic economic needs are met so that you can focus on your spiritual needs, like finding your lifelong partner.

Here are some questions you may want to ask yourself to better clarify your particular philosophy about money:

- What does money mean to you?

- How does money connect to your life purpose?

- Do you over-value or under-value money?

- Do you have debt? Or on the flip side, are you a miser?

- Does money control you?

- Do you face your money issues openly, without shame?

Though everybody's approach to money is unique, I'd like to offer some practical suggestions that seem to work well for most people:

- Pay bills today. Don't wait.

- Take care of your bills before you buy things.

- Keep debt low.

- Limit your number of credit cards—one or two is enough.

- Don't gamble with your money.

- Don't lend money unless you're willing to lose it.

- Don't buy things you don't need.

• Don't spend on items that you can't afford.

• Attend Debtors Anonymous (DA).

• Always be aware of your finances. Like the proverbial saying goes, money doesn't grow on trees!

Remember that money is really only a means to an end, whatever that "end" means for you. In any case, make sure that money serves you and not the other way around.

Taking care of your finances can go a long way toward helping you take optimum care of yourself—and you can take that to the bank!

SLOW IT DOWN!

We're always on the go, rarely taking time to slow down and "smell the roses." And where are we going, anyway, in a mad dash to the grave? Do we really have to buy into the frenetic pace of today's hurry-up society? No!

What if we made a conscious decision to slow it down instead of revving up the pace of our lives? So what if we didn't finish everything on our daily "To Do List?" What if we only checked our emails and text messages ten times a day instead of twenty? Maybe we'd have fuller lives—time to think, time to feel, and more time to love.

So, put down the cellphone, and take time to stop and smell all those beautiful, fragrant roses. And while you're at it, pick some, and give them to your partner or a friend – in person.

In other words, take the time, go with the flow, and take it slow…

Ahhhh…

BE INSPIRED!

With all the fluff and triviality of today's media circus, most of us are starving for true inspiration, to be moved to bigger and better things.

Scoop up all the inspiration you can lay your hands on. Surround yourself with empowering books and movies. Get out there and listen to public speakers that have something new and wonderful to say. Find opportunities to gratefully take in the teachings of any wise or inspiring person you come across.

Of course, that doesn't mean becoming a motivational speaker workshop junkie! Without taking action, without implementing things that you learn from these seminars into your daily life, you might as well just stay in bed!

And please tune out the manipulative ravings of all those superficial and dishonest politicians clogging up the airwaves. Turn off the TV, or at least mute those exploitative commercials. Block out anything that takes away from your sense of life purpose, your connection to your own divine reality, and feed your soul with a healthy serving of inspiration!

CREATE!

Write a book. Draw something. Paint a picture, take a picture or be in a picture. Play some music. Dance. Act in a play (because all the world's a stage!).

Find healthy ways to keep your precious connection to the Mother Earth. Get your hands dirty in the glorious terra firma and grow a lush, green garden. Help grow somebody else's garden. Create new things by yourself or with a good friend.

Be creative in the way you go about your everyday life, your daily work and your leisure activities. It's never too late to harness and actualize your own inner, creative source, your magical "inner child" and your spiritual link to life.

Make things happen, connect with everything around you and create, create, create.

BUILD FAMILY SUPPORT AND FRIENDSHIPS

The support of friends and family can be a guide and source of inspiration for taking better care of yourself. After all, we human beings were not meant to live in isolation. As I've said before, we're social beings and we have a strong inner need to connect with one another—we're wired for it.

If you don't have the luxury of supportive family and friends, seek out support in new places and social settings. You may want to connect to groups and organizations such as churches, synagogues, yoga centers and meet-up groups, just to mention a few.

Some of us will need to build relationships with others who can act as surrogate mothers, fathers, sisters, and brothers. No man is an island, and we *all* need that warm fuzzy nurturing to deflect life's inevitable slings and arrows.

SERVE OTHERS

If you really want to take care of yourself, get out of yourself and serve others.

Spiritual traditions throughout time have said that the separation between self and others is only illusion. In fact, they tell us that we are all part of the same universal fabric. These traditions also teach us that seeing ourselves in others through service closes the gap between us, allowing us to experience a richer, fuller expression of our primal link to humanity.

There are few things more healing and rewarding than aiding those in need, whether it's serving food at a homeless shelter or just lending an ear to a troubled friend. It's a great way to get up and out into the community, so I urge you to give service opportunities a try.

And you never know who you might meet—perhaps a prospective partner?

TALK TO THE ANIMALS

When it comes to living simply, effectively and happily, we could really learn a lesson from the animals. Those critters have got it all figured out. Just look at how content cats live in the moment, stretching themselves in the early morning sun. Or observe a dog's loyalty and trust, and see how it greets you with a wagging tail or happily curls up beside you at night.

Close contact with animals can lighten life's burdens and even lower blood pressure. It's no wonder that they are brought into hospitals and nursing homes to comfort the sick and the lonely. Maybe it's time to adopt a pet from your local animal shelter. Taking this loving action will help you to care for yourself by caring for another being.

Now, this doesn't mean that you become an irresponsible pet owner while satisfying your own emotional needs, as important as they may be. I knew a man who lost his wife and took in a dog for companionship. The dog became overweight, bordering on obese and almost died, simply because this man found "joy" in spoiling him with endless treats.

Remember, taking in an animal is entering into a partnership (a HMP of sorts?) with a living being that will hopefully be enriching for the both of you. So, in order to bring more joy and connection into your life, be with, talk with, and enjoy animals. They'll happily forgive your shortcomings and will always be your best friend. All they ask is that you love and care for them in return.

KEEP IT POSITIVE

An important aspect of self-care is to steer your life in a positive direction. I can't say enough about staying with the upside, because the way you view the world around you will determine your quality of life.

Those who choose to ignore the gifts and opportunities presented to them due to a negative outlook end up with nothing, at least nothing that resembles a successful relationship.

Affirmations, those positive self-statements, are a great way to keep you on track.

Here's a list of my favorites:

- Just for today, I am open to love.

- I deserve to be loved.

- I deserve a loving partnership.

- Just for today, I accept myself completely.

- I'm okay just the way I am.

- I practice self-acceptance.

- I like myself.

- I'm taking care of myself emotionally, physically and spiritually.

- I am enough.

I encourage you to write out these affirmations, say them out loud every day even if it feels uncomfortable, and see how your life changes for the better.

Another easy and accessible way to see your world more optimistically is by re-framing, consciously turning around what appears to be a bad situation and instead viewing it as beneficial or advantageous. The idea is to know that every event in your life, no matter how inconvenient or distressing it may seem, is really a gift, a lesson and an opportunity to learn. Some call it karma, others call it grace.

Last but not least, good personal boundaries offer the protection needed to maintain a healthy relationship with self and others. In order to feel safe, it's essential to know your personal needs, wants and desires, and be able to communicate them with clear and honest intention. And remember, yes means yes, and no means no.

Now, I realize that many people are afraid of telling their partners when something is bothering them, especially at first. As I've already mentioned, couples tend to be on their best behavior during the HMP and want to make a great first impression, which is understandable. But it's also important to keep the lines of communication open with your partner, even if it feels risky.

Doing all that good stuff like speaking in "I statements," limiting judgement, staying honest, showing empathy, being yourself and always keeping it positive is the way to do it.

THERAPY, COUNSELING, LIFE COACHING

Part of self-care is seeking out support, professional and otherwise, when you really need it and not buying into the social stigma that you must be crazy or weak if you do. If you need the help, get it!

When dealing with HMPs and other relationship issues, as well as thoughts, emotions, challenging life transitions or inner conflicts, there's nothing like a good therapist, counselor or life coach to help you attain that positive life perspective. It's up to you to shop around for the best helper who fits your personal style of communication and learning.

Some individuals may require a particular therapeutic technique such as cognitive-behavioral therapy or maybe a more in-depth analytical approach. One may need a more group-oriented experience while another might make better progress in a one-to-one setting. For those entering into a HMP with a new love, or for established partners who may just need a supportive jump start, couples counseling may be your best bet.

If you find yourself dealing with some deeper psychiatric issues such as unresolved trauma, clinical depression, low self-esteem, high anxiety, addiction, grief, or any kind of crisis situation that could require medication, a visit to a psychiatrist may be the way to go.

Search around, and we're sure that you'll find every kind of help under the sun. You don't have to be alone on your way to a new-and-improved program of self-care!

WORK THE 12-STEP PROGRAM OF RECOVERY

According to John Bradshaw, one of the most daring and successful social experiments of the twentieth century was the founding and incredible advancement of the 12-Step Recovery Program. Millions of people have experienced welcomed relief, true fellowship, and remarkable life changes through this innovative self-help program.

If you're dealing with addictions such as compulsive gambling, drug and alcohol abuse, Internet sex, love addiction or workaholism, a comprehensive recovery program might just be the kind of help you've been seeking. And there's probably a local 12-Step group or drug treatment center near you, should the need arise. It's always a good idea to face addiction issues within a caring community before thinking about entering into any serious love relationship.

As the 12-Steppers like to say: Keep coming back—it works if you work it, because you're worth it!

The few self-care practices that I've suggested so far, including affirming your innate worth, finding your place in the cosmos, honoring your connection to all beings, serving others and seeking help are all practical antidotes to the self-corroding shame of addiction.

MAINTAIN A SPIRITUAL PRACTICE

Whether you identify as Christian, Jewish, Buddhist, Hindu, Bahai, New Age, Born Again, Yogic, Tantric, Quaker, "spiritual but not religious," agnostic or atheist, the willingness to explore some kind of spiritual path is critical to self-care.

Soak in the profound wisdom of the great spiritual sages. Learn from and be guided by others who may have something meaningful to say.

Guru Mata Amritanandamayi, known as Amma the "Hugging Guru," says:

> *Our unselfish and compassionate acts will not only help others, but will also help to broaden our minds as well. One who picks a flower for offering is the first one to enjoy its fragrance and beauty. Likewise, it is our own self that is awakened through our selfless acts.*

Simply put, a spiritual being tends to be a more loving being, one who cares not only for self but also for all of humanity. Practice daily what speaks to your heart and soul, for this is your way to serenity and your truth.

LAUGH LOUDLY AND OFTEN!

Laughter is the best medicine and a powerful spiritual practice in itself. It'll keep you alive by reducing stress and will add something positive to your day-to-day existence.

Laughter is an enjoyable and effective way to promote happiness and good feelings all around. Sharing your humor with others can help to ease the sting of life's tough challenges and scary inevitabilities.

As the late satirist, Kurt Vonnegut once said, "Laughter and tears are both responses to frustration and exhaustion. I myself prefer to laugh, since there is less cleaning to do afterward."

So tell a joke, laugh at yourself often, and don't take life too seriously.

With that in mind, I leave you with one more quote that really says it all, from the astute and wizened soul of John Bradshaw:

"Total self-love and acceptance is the only foundation for happiness and the love of others."

Chapter 11
Honeymoon Phase Success

"Know where to find the information and how to use it. That's the secret of success."

—Albert Einstein

"Communication is important; it links the hearts of two, together, making them understand what each other means."

—Anonymous

We've come a long way on our journey by way of the HMP, learning the basic understanding of how it relates to long-term love. We've also discussed its different aspects by including the cultural, biological and gender-specific issues surrounding relationships—all integral parts to finding love and keeping love.

The keys to a successful HMP lie in self-care, self-acceptance and the understanding that relationships are evolving partnerships requiring constant care and renewal. By living in the moment and practicing effective communication, you're giving yourself a great start at generating a positive beginning to a promising and hopefully lasting love relationship.

But a successful HMP may also require the courage to face some tough issues such as a difficult past, or shame-related issues like addiction and abuse, so love can freely grow, unencumbered.

Enjoy the process, bask in it and drink it up, but also approach this crucial time with mindful caution. There's no reason to needlessly invite emotional pain into your life when you can avoid it. I can't stress enough that the HMP needs to be approached with mindfulness and self-knowledge, and not entered into as a frivolous or mindless game of chance.

Even if you feel yourself caught up in that initial swirl of HMP passion, excitement and high hopes, I encourage you to boldly take that risk of love, but with your head on straight. The HMP needs to be continuously celebrated and fully experienced, not as something to be passed through as a quick means to an end, but as a vital bridge to everlasting love.

EIGHTEEN CONTEMPLATIONS FOR HMP REALIZATION

Here are some concluding thoughts that will hopefully help you to apply all that I've discussed in the preceding chapters to help you on your way to ultimate HMP success:

1. Learn who you are and who they are. Are you compatible with one another? Do you share the same basic values? Answering these questions can take some time, because knowing yourself and your prospective partner is a gradual process not to be rushed into or taken lightly.

2. There's an anonymous saying, "Love is communication, and a lack of communication is a lack of love." So, express your love by openly communicating your hopes, dreams, needs and wants to your partner, right from the beginning. You'll never go wrong with clear and direct communication.

3. Don't create unrealistic expectations, but do promote mutual understanding, even agreements about what each is expecting from the relationship. Surprises are great, but you don't want to be emotionally blindsided.

4. Always view your partner as an equal, whether you're just beginning your journey of love or you've been with your partner for decades. Love has to exist on an equal playing field.

5. Two halves may make a whole, but two whole individuals make a successful partnership. I'm talking about the importance of relationship unity and personal integrity. Too many people attempt to fix themselves by attaching onto another person, instead of striving to become complete beings unto themselves first.

6. Honesty is the best policy. You have to be honest with yourself and your partner about what you're feeling and experiencing in the moment. Don't be phony or insincere, and above all, don't mislead yourself or your partner. If you make promises to each other, honor and keep them. It's never attractive to go back on your word—and

that's no lie!

7. You don't have to hide if you're unhappy or hurt by something your partner might've said or done. I know so many friends and clients who do this, thinking that it's better not to rock the relationship boat. Even I've been guilty of that!

8. Couples counseling early in the relationship is always a good idea, even if you're off to a flying start. Anything that helps build a foundation of mutual trust and goodwill is a great way to begin a loving relationship.

9. If you're experiencing grief or any burning issues from the past, deal with them sensibly. Do your best not to project your fear, rage, or shame onto your significant other. Instead, bring your woes to a trusted friend or professional in order to take the emotional heat off your partner. Share some of your suffering with your mate, but only when appropriate. Nothing kills a promising love relationship like overbearing anguish.

10. Do not be overly possessive. Give plenty of physical and emotional space to your prospective partner. Allow him or her to freely step back from the relationship or even leave it, if necessary. Hostage-taking is a surefire deal breaker at any stage of a love relationship. Let it all flow naturally without the need to hold on too tightly, because controlling behavior is not loving behavior and inevitably sabotages love.

11. The HMP experience will be more successful if each partner has a supportive, already-established network of family and friends. Keep your support systems intact and seek them out, especially when you really need them.

12. When finding or keeping love, don't stop what you're doing in your life. Keep up with your usual hobbies and interests, the ones that make you happy. Chances are, your partner will like and respect you more for having your own fulfilling life.

13. Support each other. Share the burdens but always take individual responsibility for your own actions. A successful relationship is always a two-way street.

14. Be spontaneous and maintain an open-minded, pioneering spirit with your new love interest. Share your wonder and excitement. It's a lot more interesting that way.

15. Let love in and don't deny it when it happens. Allow yourself to be nurtured, even shamelessly pampered, because you deserve it and so does your partner.

16. As we all know, sexuality and physical attraction are essential and anticipated parts of every loving relationship. It's okay for you to be physically turned on to your new or current partner. Conversely, if one becomes overwhelmed by sexual cravings, it can cloud re-

ality and potentially be destructive. So be mindful of the other's needs and wants without letting things like physical drives, though natural enough, get in the way of love. And for crying out loud, keep guilt out of it!

17. Clear thinking and assertive action are what's needed to build a healthy relationship. If you want to create that solid bond with another person, avoid all unnecessary distractions, obsessive thinking and compulsive behaviors, because they are the fuel for such things as addictions, the unholy forces that will habitually undermine and destroy love.

18. See your HMP for what it is, how it presents itself, and how it progresses—emotionally, physically, intellectually and spiritually. As I always like to say, know your partner and yourself.

LOVE BONDING—THE BEST OF ALL WORLDS

The above ideas are the brick and mortar for effective communication and positive interactions found within all successful HMP's. Once this foundation has been built, you and your partner can use it as a realistic transition into something even more extraordinary—long-term love.

So use the power of your deepest convictions and be open to your partner's core beliefs in order to take your relationship to new heights. You just might find that the creation of a true loving bond is the best of all worlds. I also encourage you to be receptive, without prior judgment, to the spiritual aspects of finding and keeping love.

And speaking of spirituality…

EPILOGUE
A Divine Honeymoon Forever

"By night on my bed I sought him whom my soul loveth."

—"Song of Songs" (3:1)

"Love doesn't sit there, like a stone; it has to be made, like bread; remade all the time, made new."

—Ursula K.

So here we are, well downriver.

We've spoken a lot about what the HMP is and is not, about preparing yourself for new love, and how it directly relates to successful lifelong intimacy with another person as well as a broader awareness of self.

You may have noticed that there are a lot of parallels between the path to love and the spiritual path. It's no coincidence that almost every major religion in the world considers the bond of love—including marriage—to be holy, something highly spiritual and sacred that transcends the secular world. Actually, the two are routinely seen as almost one and the same.

Spirituality, as it relates to the HMP, closely follows our characterization of successful, healthy love relationships discussed earlier in this book. It involves a constant revitalization, a continual "showing up" that allows each participant to be part of a collaborative union, a co-creation. And this involves the ability to see one another as already complete spiritual beings.

Once you experience true intimacy with yourself—the prerequisite for any healthy relationship—and *then* join with another, you'll have a better opportunity to include spirituality into your new or existing relationship.

Successful love relationships aren't just about two people meeting and spending time together. They're about individuals going beyond themselves to create and reach for something larger. When your relationship develops this way, both of you are in direct line to experience a more profound and transcendent form of love.

This "looking beyond oneself" allows for mutual tapping into something even more mighty and mysterious, which may include devotion to a spiritual entity. This could be a higher power, or a belief in, as Juan Castenada the desert mystic called it, a "separate reality."

Some say that spirituality can only be found in the present moment. The creation and nurturance of love is about the here and now, not some futuristic, pie-in-the-sky fantasy. This is not meant to contradict our firm belief that the HMP can last a lifetime. But you'll need to focus, as those 12-Steppers would say, on making it happen "one day at a time."

The HMP encompasses many other spiritual ideas like hope, mindfulness, connection, universality, awareness, willingness, serenity, openness, wonderment, beauty, bliss, kindness, compassion, infatuation, the nascent state, and of course, love. And the splendid list goes on and on.

Like everything else in life, the HMP is always in a state of flux, but always with an eye on the creation and extension of mutual love. Perhaps the Sufi mystic and poet, Rumi, said it best by using "the beloved" as a means to examine one's sacred relationship with the divine: "Day and night, I see the face of union—I am the mirror of God."

The passionate force of his constant adoration of the beloved should be familiar to anyone who's ever been swept away by the powerful emotions felt for a lover.

But, as we've been saying all along, the idea is to first harness this awesome power with right knowledge and a deep-seeded love of self, while maintaining a high level of love and respect for one another. Whether with a new lover or an established partner, we need to preserve our wholeness of self, and that takes mindful effort and discipline.

Take Tantra, the Eastern spiritual system of harnessing sexual energy for the purpose of personal expansion and loving union with the divine (Tantra literally means "to stretch or expand"). This highly spiritual practice requires daily discipline and sustained effort.

The practice of yoga also involves a steady and focused determination. Who ever thought that attending a single yoga class would bring you to enlightenment, let alone give you that perfect body? Likewise, it would be just as foolish to believe that a life-long romance happens overnight.

Lasting love involves a conscious decision of giving yourself to a process that can move you forward on your spiritual path—a path that takes time, is constantly changing and always evolving. This process, if approached wisely and with perseverance, will lead you to ultimate fulfillment and eternal union with your beloved.

When you enter into connection with another human being, you're also dealing with an incredible life force that can either propel you into a beautifully balanced relationship or can cause you to lose yourself in the process. This kind of loss may ultimately destroy the love relationship you had hoped for and lead you to lose sight of your spiritual path. That's where self-care and self-love come into play.

And that's what spirituality and positive love relationships are all about: creating a sense of oneness that calls for constant acts of re-creation in order to form a true spiritual union with another person. In the same way, the promise of a wonderful partnership is achieved through the steady process of creating and sustaining love. You need to keep showing up and continuously renew your commitment, one day, one moment at a time.

But, as I've always believed, you've got to be nearly complete within yourself before a true spiritual connection can be reached. It just doesn't work for two lovers to think of themselves as separate parts of a couple. Rather, each one needs to strive for individual wholeness and *then* come together to form something greater.

This notion of connection to something beyond the self, to something as mysterious as Universal Consciousness, the Unknowable or even God, is something worthy of striving for in this lifetime. After all, isn't a gradual merging with the universe really where it's at? Many gurus and mystics would say that this striving for cosmic oneness is our ultimate goal in life.

Once you internalize this deeper understanding about the illusion of separateness, a separateness which can only block the way to a true uniting of hearts, then you're ready for something wonderful and profound, a true and enduring experience of love. With this spiritual realization comes the power to create and re-create the partnership for which you've always hoped for—the actualization of eternal love.

So, I wish you all the best in your loving endeavors, and remember that you have the innate capability to achieve true intimacy with yourself, your partner and all that exists. Stay positive, be mindful, be creative, practice self-care, keep showing up and stick to the challenge of creating, nurturing and finally tasting the fruits of lasting love.

Use your divinely given intelligence, but stay true to your emotions, and humbly pay close attention to all the universe has to offer and teach you. Do not be discouraged if love isn't right on time, for great civilizations and great partnerships were never created in a single day. Finding and keeping love is a process requiring patience and a steadfast belief that those original elements of the HMP—that first encounter with love—can last a lifetime.

So tap into your deep well of personal power with renewed confidence and a light heart, and calmly drift along with the natural flow of this wondrous river we call life as it empties into the vast sea of abiding love, and beyond. Believe in the enduring power of love as you joyfully experience the creative and incredible regenerative power of the Honeymoon Phase—the ultimate pathway to eternal love and your Honeymoon Forever!

AFTERWORD
One Final Gem...

I leave you with something simple yet uplifting, something that will help you stay inspired and committed to your journey to true love. It is a hopeful prayer for a loving and everlasting union, right from the huge heart of Rumi:

May these vows and this marriage be blessed.

May it be sweet milk, this marriage, like wine and halva.

May this marriage offer fruit and shade like the date palm.

May this marriage be full of laughter, our every day a day in paradise.

May this marriage be a sign of compassion,

A seal of happiness here and hereafter.

May this marriage have a fair face and a good name,

An omen as welcome as the moon in a clear blue sky.

I am out of words to describe how spirit mingles in this marriage.

AMEN

REFERENCES

CHAPTER 1

1) Herb Goldberg, Ph.D. *The Inner Male*, Overcoming roadblocks to Intimacy, New York: Nash Publishing Corporation, 1976, p. 5
2) Dr. Susan Campbell, *The Couple's Journey*, "Five Stages of Relationships", 1980
3) Nancy Wesson, Ph.D. Online Article; "Stages of a Healthy Relationship"
4) John Bradshaw, Santa Fe Lecture, Self & Family Conference, 2007
5) John Gray, *Men Are From Mars, Women Are from Venus*, A Practical Guide for Improving Communication and Getting What You Want in Your Relationships, New York: Harper Collins Publishers, 1992, p. 286
6) Gay Hendricks, Ph.D.& Kathlyn Hendricks, Ph.D., *Conscious Loving*, The Journey to Co-Commitment, New York, Bantam Books, 1990, p.18

CHAPTER 2

1) Nancy Wesson, Ph.D., Article: "Is it possible to remain special to each other even after several years of being together as a couple?", www.wespsych.com.

CHAPTER 3

1) Nancy Wesson, Ph.D., Article: "Is it possible to remain special to each

other even after several years of being together as a couple?", www.we-spsych.com.
2) Woody Allen: *Annie Hall*, United Artists, Release date: April 20th, 1977.

CHAPTER 4

1) Ram Dass, Magazine Interview, Truly Alive; An Overview of the book, *Be Love Now,* Jan/Feb, 2011.
2) Dr. Gerald Jampolsky, *Love is Letting Go of Fear*, pps. 17, 36, 51, 65.
3) John Bradshaw, Public Lecture, L.A., including, "Four Stages of Mature Love", 2004.
4) Erich Fromm, *The Art of Loving*, 1956, p.5.
5) Elaine Hatfield & Walster,
6) Dr. William Jankowiak, "A Cross-Cultural Perspective On Romantic Love", Ethnology, p.150, 1992 (Quote)
7) CS Lewis, *The Four Loves*, p.20
8) Dr. Scott Peck, *The Road Less Traveled: A New Psychology of Love,* Traditional Values and Spiritual Growth, New York: Simon & Schuster Inc., 1978.
9) Dr. Bianco Acevedo (CUNY Stony Brook Study)
10) Helen Gurley Brown, Having It All: New York: Simon & Shuster, Linden Press, NY, 1982, Chapter 8, pps. 253-254

CHAPTER 5

1) Dr. M.R. Liebowitz (Psychiatrist), 1983
2) Dr. Helen Fisher, *Why We Love:* The Nature and Chemistry of Romantic Love, New York: Henry Holt & Company, 2004.
3) Prof/Dr. Norma McCoy, SF State
4) Tobias Esch & George Stefano, The Neurobiology of Love, June, 2005
5) Larry J. Young, "*The Neural Basis of Pair Bonding in a Monogamous Species:* A Model for Understanding the Biological Basis of Human Behavior": Where?, Year? pps. 91-103.

6) Hatfield, E. & Walster, G. W *A New Look at Love*. Lanham, MD: University Press of America, 1985.
7) Andreas Bartels & Semir Zeki, The Neural Basis of Romantic Love, London College, England, 2000.
8) Donatella Marazziti & G.B. Cassano, "The Neurobiology of Attraction", Pisa, Italy, 2003.

CHAPTER 6

1) Francesco Alberoni, *Falling in Love,*
2) Susan Sprecher, Quintin Sullivan, and Elaine Hatfield, "*Mate Selection Preferences:* Gender Differences Examined in a National Sample", Journal of Personality and Social Psychology, 1994, p. 1079.

CHAPTER 8

1) D.H. Lowenherz, *The 50 Greatest Love Letters Of All Time,*
2) D.H.Lowenherz., p.91
3) John Bowlby, Online Article: "Attachment Theory".
4) Matt, Recovering Addict, Sex & Love Addiction Big Book.
5) Pia Mellody, *Facing Love Addiction:* Giving Yourself the Power to Change the Way You Love, New York: Harper Collins Publishers, Inc., 2003, p.60.
6) Anne Wilson Schaef, *Escape From Intimacy:* Untangling the 'Love' Addictions: Sex, Romance, Relationships. New York, Harper Collins Publishers, 1989.
7) Brenda Schaffer, *Signs of Addiction*, "Signs of Addictive Love", Hazelden
8) John Gray, *Men Are From Mars, Women Are From Venus*, p.284
9) Jon Bradshaw quote: *Healing the Shame That Binds You*, p.vii

CHAPTER 9

1) David H. Lowenherz, The 50 Greatest Love Letters of All Time: New

York: Gramercy Books, 2002.
2) Melody Beattie, *The New Codependency*, Help & Guidance for Today's Generation: New York: Simon & Schuster, 2009, p. 21.Cervantes, *Don Quixote*
3) Abraham Maslow, "Hierarchy of Needs"

If you enjoyed *Honeymoon Forever,* consider this fiction work by the author:

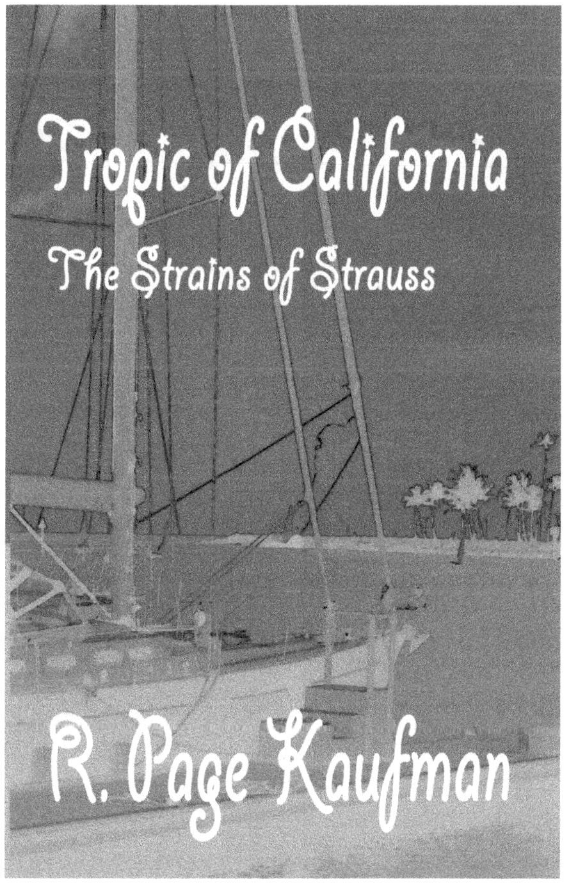

Join definitive tragic character Alan Strauss on a rapidly unfolding satirical romp through glitzy Southern California. This twenty seven year-old divorced ex-shoe salesman and "life survivor," temporarily down on his luck, is suddenly lifted up to a high corporate position and offered riches beyond belief. Yet through a stunning twist of fate, Alan learns the true meaning of love and friendship. "Tropic of California" is an entertaining, humorous, and romantic (yes, romantic) look at the human condition.

and the accompanying music CD by the author:

Ten selections of contemporary trombone jazz from his prior CD entitled "Sunday Drive." Featuring Robert Page Kaufman (R. Page Kaufman) on trombone; Grant Gelssman, Eric Marienthal, Bobby Rodriguez, Bill Liston, Dave Carpenter, Bob Feldman, Domenic Genova, Ron Aston, Jon Ferraro, Bob Leatherbarrow and Luis Conte accompanying.

About the Author

Contemporary satirist and native Californian R. Page Kaufman was born, raised and schooled in Los Angeles. His experience as a psychotherapist gives him unique insight into both the humorous and tragic side of the human condition and its various interesting manifestations within the Southern California Lifestyle. Multi-award-winning author of numerous socio-political essays, he is particularly interested in human communication and love relationships. He is currently living in New Mexico, in his words, "taking a well-earned break from the L. A. freeways."

If you enjoyed *Honeymoon Forever,* consider these other fine books from Savant Books and Publications:

Essay, Essay, Essay by Yasuo Kobachi
Aloha from Coffee Island by Walter Miyanari
Footprints, Smiles and Little White Lies by Daniel S. Janik
The Illustrated Middle Earth by Daniel S. Janik
Last and Final Harvest by Daniel S. Janik
A Whale's Tale by Daniel S. Janik
Tropic of California by R. Page Kaufman
Tropic of California (the companion music CD) by R. Page Kaufman
The Village Curtain by Tony Tame
Dare to Love in Oz by William Maltese
The Interzone by Tatsuyuki Kobayashi
Today I Am a Man by Larry Rodness
The Bahrain Conspiracy by Bentley Gates
Called Home by Gloria Schumann
First Breath edited by Z. M. Oliver
The Jumper Chronicles by W. C. Peever
William Maltese's Flicker - #1 Book of Answers by William Maltese
My Unborn Child by Orest Stocco
Last Song of the Whales by Four Arrows
Perilous Panacea by Ronald Klueh
Falling but Fulfilled by Zachary M. Oliver
Mythical Voyage by Robin Ymer
Hello, Norma Jean by Sue Dolleris
Charlie No Face by David B. Seaburn
Number One Bestseller by Brian Morley
My Two Wives and Three Husbands by S. Stanley Gordon
In Dire Straits by Jim Currie
Wretched Land by Mila Komarnisky
Who's Killing All the Lawyers? by A. G. Hayes
Ammon's Horn by G. Amati
Wavelengths edited by Zachary M. Oliver
Communion by Jean Blasiar and Jonathan Marcantoni
The Oil Man by Leon Puissegur
Random Views of Asia from the Mid-Pacific by William E. Sharp

The Isla Vista Crucible by Reilly Ridgell
Blood Money by Scott Mastro
In the Himalayan Nights by Anoop Chandola
On My Behalf by Helen Doan
Chimney Bluffs by David B. Seaburn
The Loons by Sue Dolleris
Light Surfer by David Allan Williams
The Judas List by A. G. Hayes
Path of the Templar—Book 2 of The Jumper Chronicles by W. C. Peever
The Desperate Cycle by Tony Tame
Shutterbug by Buz Sawyer
Blessed are the Peacekeepers by Tom Donnelly and Mike Munger
Bellwether Messages edited by D. S. Janik
The Turtle Dances by Daniel S. Janik
The Lazarus Conspiracies by Richard Rose
Purple Haze by George B. Hudson
Imminent Danger by A. G. Hayes
Lullaby Moon (CD) by Malia Elliott of Leon & Malia
Volutions edited by Suzanne Langford
In the Eyes of the Son by Hans Brinckmann
The Hanging of Dr. Hanson by Bentley Gates
Flight of Destiny by Francis Powell
Elaine of Corbenic by Tima Z. Newman
Ballerina Birdies by Marina Yamamoto
More More Time by David B. Seabird
Crazy Like Me by Erin Lee
Cleopatra Unconquered by Helen R. Davis
Valedictory by Daniel Scott
The Chemical Factor by A. G. Hayes
Quantum Death by A. G. Hayes and Raymond Gaynor
Big Heaven by Charlotte Hebert
Captain Riddle's Treasure by GV Rama Rao
All Things Await by Seth Clabough
Tsunami Libido by Cate Burns
Finding Kate by A. G. Hayes
The Adventures of Purple Head, Buddha Monkey... by Erik/Forest Bracht
In the Shadows of My Mind by Andrew Massie
The Gumshoe by Richard Rose
In Search of Somatic Therapy by Setsuko Tsuchiya
Cereus by Z. Roux
The Solar Triangle by A. G. Hayes
Shadow and Light edited by Helen R. Davis
A Real Daughter by Lynne McKelvey

StoryTeller by Nicholas Bylotas
Bo Henry at Three Forks by Daniel Bradford
Kindred edited by Gary "Doc" Krinberg
Cleopatra Victorious by Helen R. Davis
Navel of the Sea by Elizabeth McKague
Entwined edited by Gary "Doc" Krinberg
Critical Writing: Stories as Phenomena by Jamie Dela Cruz
Truth and Tell Travel the Solar System by Helen R. Davis
Aloha La'a Kea edited by Robert "Uhene" Maikai
Hawaii Kids Music Vol 1 by Leon and Malia
William Maltese's Flicker - #2 Book of Ascendency by William Maltese

Coming Soon
Hawaii Kids Music Vol 2 by Leon and Malia
The Power of Dance by Setsuko Tsuchiya
I Love Liking You A Lot by Greg Hatala
Retribution by Richard Rose
Shep's Adventures by George Hudson
Lion's Way by Rita Ariyoshi

http://www.savantbooksandpublications.com

R Page Kaufman

and from our *avant garde* imprint, Aignos Publishing:

The Dark Side of Sunshine by Paul Guzzo
Cazadores de Libros Perdidos by German William Cabasssa Barber [Spanish]
The Desert and the City by Derek Bickerton
The Overnight Family Man by Paul Guzzo
There is No Cholera in Zimbabwe by Zachary M. Oliver
John Doe by Buz Sawyers
The Piano Tuner's Wife by Jean Yamasaki Toyama
An Aura of Greatness by Brendan P. Burns
Polonio Pass by Doc Krinberg
Iwana by Alvaro Leiva
University and King by Jeffrey Ryan Long
The Surreal Adventures of Dr. Mingus by Jesus Richard Felix Rodriguez
Letters by Buz Sawyers
In the Heart of the Country by Derek Bickerton
El Camino De Regreso by Maricruz Acuna [Spanish]
Prepositions by Jean Yamasaki Toyama
Deep Slumber of Dogs by Doc Krinberg
Saddam's Parrot by Jim Currie
Beneath Them by Natalie Roers
Chang the Magic Cat by A. G. Hayes
Illegal by E. M. Duesel
Island Wildlife: Exiles, Expats and Exotic Others by Robert Friedman
The Winter Spider by Doc Krinberg
The Princess in My Head by J. G. Matheny
Comic Crusaders by Richard Rose
I'll Remember by Clif McCrady
The City and the Desert by Derek Bickerton
The Edge of Madness by Raymond Gaynor
'Til Then Our Written Love Will Have to Do by Cheri Woods

http://www.savantbooksandpublications.com

www.ingramcontent.com/pod-product-compliance
Lightning Source LLC
LaVergne TN
LVHW010915110826
845149LV00013B/2370

* 9 7 8 0 9 9 9 6 9 3 8 2 7 *